THE BEST VERSION OF YOU

DAVID COOPER

THE BEST VERSION OF YOU

DAVID COOPER

Director of Publications: David W. Ray
Managing Editor of Publications: Lance Colkmire
Copy Editor: Esther Metaxas
Editorial Assistant: Elaine McDavid
Graphic Layout: Shelia Stewart

ISBN: 978-1-64288-307-7

Copyright © 2023 by Pathway Press
1080 Montgomery Avenue
Cleveland, Tennessee 37311

Visit *www.pathwaypress.org* for more information.

CONTENTS

INTRODUCTION

My pastor used to say, "The worse the world is without, the deeper we need to go within." Our strength of character enables us to deal with the stress of circumstances. The Apostle Paul wrote: "Therefore we do not lose heart. Though outwardly we are wasting away, yet inwardly we are being renewed day by day" (2 Corinthians 4:16).

The Christian life is lived from the inside out. When we are born again by faith in Jesus, the presence and power of God resides within us through the Holy Spirit. "Don't you realize that your body is the temple of the Holy Spirit, who lives in you?" (1 Corinthians 6:19 NLT). The Spirit of God empowers us and transforms us from the inside out. When the world within you changes, the world around you will start to change. Your current life situation merely reflects what's in your heart. The world within us—attitudes, values, and beliefs—plays a key role in creating the world around us.

The Holy Spirit produces in our hearts the fruit of the Spirit, which are nine attributes of Christ's image in us. These nine attributes will enrich and empower you to live your best life. "The fruit of the Spirit is love, joy, peace, patience, kindness, goodness, faithfulness, gentleness and self-control. Against such things there is no law" (Galatians 5:22-23).

There is no law or principle that can defeat a person who expresses the fruit of the Spirit. The fruit grows from the inside out, from the heart to the world around you. The fruit of the Spirit will enrich your personality, character, mood, attitude, communications, and relationships. That's your best self.

It is my prayer for you that as you read this book you will grow spiritually in the quality and quantity of the fruit that only comes from the Holy Spirit. You will become a better person, your relationships will get better, and your life situation will get better as the fruit of the Spirit is produced in you from the inside out. Thanks for reading!

—Dr. David Cooper

1
ALL YOU NEED IS LOVE

Love is the ageless theme of artists and authors, poets and philosophers, music and movies. One of the most famous love songs in pop-culture history is The Beatles' "All You Need Is Love." It's true—all you need is love!

Your best self is described in the fruit of the Spirit. "The fruit of the Spirit is love, joy, peace, patience, kindness, goodness, faithfulness, gentleness and self-control" (Galatians 5:22-23). These nine attributes are the result of the work of the Holy Spirit in our lives. As we grow spiritually in our relationship with Christ, we bear spiritual fruit. People can see the image of Christ in us!

Love is the predominant quality of the character of Christ in us. The other fruit are expressions of love. "Now these three remain: faith, hope, and love—but the greatest of these is love" (1 Corinthians 13:13 CSB). Love is the greatest emotion. Love is the greatest thought. Love is the greatest action. Love is the greatest motive and the greatest command. "The whole law can be summed up in this one command: 'Love your neighbor as yourself'"

(Galatians 5:14 NLT). Love is the greatest attribute of God. "God is love" (1 John 4:8). The word *love* sums up all the attributes of divinity and the image of God in us.

Life on the inside affects everything on the outside. To improve the world around us, we start by improving the world within us. As Christians we desire real change on the inside so we become more like Jesus. The grace of God that's on the inside comes out for others to see! Our behavior reflects our beliefs. Our character correlates with our convictions. Our virtues match our values.

Work Versus Fruit

The fruit of the Holy Spirit stands in contrast to the works of the flesh, or the sinful nature. "Live by the Spirit, and you will not gratify the desires of the sinful nature" (Galatians 5:16). The battle of the flesh and spirit is the conflict that wars within us all. "For the flesh desires what is against the Spirit, and the Spirit desires what is against the flesh; these are opposed to each other, so that you don't do what you want" (Galatians 5:17 CSB). We want to do good but often don't do it because the flesh defeats us. The word *flesh* means "the sinful nature with its desires and impulses." The flesh is the dark side of human nature and the lower nature that results from sin. The flesh is the immoral and immature part of our nature.

Jesus redeems us from sin and gives us a new nature so we "participate in the divine nature and escape the corruption in the world caused by evil desires" (2 Peter 1:4). We're born again! As a new creation in Christ, we grow spiritually so we can overcome the flesh and live by the Spirit. Jesus *delivers* us from the flesh, but He doesn't *destroy* it; that's why we struggle with the flesh. We feel the inner conflict between the flesh and the Spirit.

The fruit of the Spirit stands in sharp contrast to the works of the flesh. They are completely opposite and diametrically opposed to one another. "The acts of the sinful nature are obvious: sexual immorality, impurity and debauchery; idolatry and witchcraft; hatred, discord, jealousy, fits of rage, selfish ambition, dissensions, factions and envy; drunkenness, orgies, and the like. I warn you, as I did before, that those who live like this will not inherit the kingdom of God" (Galatians 5:19-21). That's why Jesus said, "You must be born again" (John 3:7). Only God's saving grace can redeem us from the flesh so we can produce the fruit of the Spirit. When we do, others see Christ in us the hope of glory! The works of the flesh describes the worst life, while the fruit of the Spirit describes the best life.

Fruit is very different from work. Fruit grows naturally, but work takes effort. When you plant a tree, it automatically bears fruit. You have to nurture the tree, but a healthy tree bears fruit all by itself. A healthy Christian naturally produces spiritual fruit. If you grow in faith, you will bear the fruit of the Spirit. Spiritual growth results in the spiritual fruit of Christlike character. Fruit comes naturally from the quality of the tree. Jesus said, "[A] good tree bears good fruit" (Matthew 7:17). When we're born again through faith in Jesus and our sins are forgiven and our hearts are cleansed, we have a new nature that produces the fruit of the Spirit. "If anyone is in Christ, he is a new creation" (2 Corinthians 5:17). As we grow spiritually, we will produce the fruit of the Spirit.

Love Divine

The greatest attribute of a Christlike life is love. So, what is this love? The fruit of the Spirit is not your effort but rather the work of the Holy Spirit in you. The Greeks used four different words to describe types of love. *Eros* is passionate, emotional, and romantic love. *Storgē* refers to family love and, especially, love and care for children. I grew up in a great family. We did everything together as a family. Those of us who are blessed with great families know the meaning of *storgē* and how powerful and amazing a great family is. The church is "the family of believers" (Galatians 6:10). The third Greek word for love is *philia*, meaning "brotherly love, fondness, and friendship." It's the root of the word *Philadelphia*, "The City of Brotherly Love." "A friend loves at all times" (Proverbs 17:17).

The fruit of the Spirit is not *eros*, *storgē*, or *philia*, but *agape*. The Greek philosophers said *agape* is a divine love that is higher and greater than any other kind of love. Historians tell us early Greek authors didn't use the word *agape* because it was so transcendent and we aren't capable of loving like that. *Agape*, they said, was divine love.

Agape, they thought, was beyond our human capacity. However, when the apostles wrote the New Testament, they used *agape* almost exclusively to not only describe the nature of God and the work of Christ, but also the essential quality of the Christian life. God's nature and actions are purely those of love. Love is God's only motive: "God so loved the world that he gave his one and only Son" (John 3:16). The Apostle Paul said, "The Son of God . . . loved me and gave Himself for me" (Galatians 2:20 NKJV).

The Holy Spirit produces divine love in us so we can love others as God loves. Divinity now flows through our humanity, producing the fruit of the Spirit. The mysterious love the Greeks believed existed in the universe is found in Jesus! By grace, we can love with agape. Jesus is the incarnation of the love of God. He is in us and He gives us the power to love as He loves. We are capable of loving others with the love of God because we have a new nature through the new birth.

The fruit of the Spirit is the unconditional love of God in us. When Jesus delivers us from self-centeredness, we can love as God created us to love. Sin keeps us from being what God created us to be. "If anyone acknowledges that Jesus is the Son of God, God lives in him and he in God. And so we know and rely on the love God has for us. God is love. Whoever lives in love lives in God, and God in him" (1 John 4:15-16).

How is that possible? We can love because we are born again, and the Holy Spirit creates the spiritual fruit of love in us. He changes our nature. He gives us the gift of agape. He gives us the power and the ability to love. Once you're born again, you will recognize a change in your life and you'll become more and more loving toward people. Spiritual maturity means growing in love. "God has poured out his love into our hearts by the Holy Spirit, whom he has given us" (Romans 5:5). God's grace and power enable us to love as He loves us.

Love on Demand

Agape is a unique love because it operates on demand. So, God commands us to love. Jesus said, "A new command I give you that you love one another as I have loved you" (see John 13:34). He wouldn't command us to do something that we can't do. "I can do all things through Christ who strengthens me" (Philippians 4:13 NKJV). I can love because Christ gives me strength. You and I can love others with the love of God! That makes agape different from emotional love. While agape includes emotions of compassion, mercy, and devotion, it is also a decision. Agape chooses to love out of obedience to Christ.

Agape is not governed by emotions but by choice. So, when we get mad, hurt, or disappointed, we don't lash out in rage. Instead, we choose to forgive and to show mercy. The power of agape is why Jesus could pray for God to forgive the soldiers who crucified Him and the leaders who condemned Him. He transcended His feelings and chose to forgive His enemies! Jesus prayed, "Father, forgive them, for they don't know what they are doing" (Luke 23:34 NLT). Christ in us gives us the power to do the same thing in our reactions to what people may say or do against us.

Jesus' command to love comes with the capability to keep the command. Emotional love can't be commanded because it's a feeling, albeit a powerful one. Feelings come and go, rise and fall, and do what they want to do with little rhyme or reason. None of us can really control our emotions. We wish we could, but we can't. Feelings fluctuate for no apparent reason and it's difficult to manage them.

We are victims of our emotions. You can't command someone to fall in love with you. Falling in love is magical and mysterious. We don't even know why it happens. You've probably had someone fall in love with you, but you didn't feel the same way about them, and you can't make yourself fall in love. Eros is mysterious.

You've also probably been hurt in a relationship because you fell in love with someone, but they didn't feel the same way. You dated for a while and got your hopes up for a long-term relationship. Then, the other person broke off the relationship. You get the friend speech: "I just want to be friends." That's code for *it's over*! Or you get the time speech: "I just need some time to sort out my feelings." Or, worse, this excuse: "I need some space." That means you're about to orbit out of the relationship. No matter how hard you work to get somebody to fall in love with you, you can't because eros doesn't function by demand. But agape does!

Agape is spiritual love. Regardless of how upset or angry you are with someone, you have the ability to override those feelings and act in love. Regardless of how you feel, you're not the victim of your feelings. You may be hurt, disappointed, or angry. As a Christian, you can override those negative feelings and show kindness, compassion, and forgiveness. You don't have to be the victim of negative emotions. You can choose to love others in spite of what they have done to you. Jesus said, "Greater love has no one than this, that he lay down his life for his friends" (John 15:13). Agape is the power to "lay down" your feelings and to forgive.

Agape is the key to Christian marriage. "Husbands, love [agape] your wives, just as Christ loved [agape] the church and gave himself up for her" (Ephesians 5:25). You see, agape is a selfless love; it puts others first. It is a serving love; it doesn't try to dominate and rule. It finds joy being a servant, not being lord. It's also a sacrificial love. Love gives up the things we want so others can get the things they need. When we love, we put others ahead of ourselves.

Feel the Best

Agape has three different aspects—the way we feel, the way we think, and the way we act. Agape is a feeling of mercy, compassion, and empathy for others. We hurt with others. We share their grief. We share their pain. We're concerned about the welfare of others who are less fortunate. When Jesus saw the crowds, He was moved with compassion (Matthew 14:14). Love makes us stop and do something to help those in need.

The new nature of agape is empathetic and non-judgmental. We are not harsh and rude. We feel sympathetic for people going through tough times. We're not calloused. The word *compassion* means to hurt for others at a gut-level. It comes from the Greek word for the intestines to describe gut-level pain. Jesus could feel the fear and confusion of the crowds of people who came to hear Him preach good news and teach a higher way of life in the kingdom of God. They were looking for real spiritual answers and fulfillment. So, He was moved with compassion. He preached the kingdom of God because He cared about people, which is the only pure motive for any ministry we do. That's agape. God gives us that gift of love when we are born again through faith in Christ. Have you felt in your gut the love of God well up in you like a mighty river that moved you with compassion to help others in need?

In His story of the Good Samaritan, Jesus describes a man who was robbed, beaten, and left in a ditch. The priest walked by and saw the man lying there, but he kept on walking to the Temple. The Levite, who worked for the priest, also saw the man but he too passed by to go to the Temple to do his religious duty. But the Samaritan took pity on the helpless man. He, like Jesus, was moved with compassion. He did what he did because love motivated him. Love made him stop and help. He saved the injured man, bandaged his wounds, took him to an inn, and paid for him to stay there until he recovered. Compassion takes action! That's agape.

Think the Best

When we love with agape, we think the best about others and believe in their potential. Love looks at others through the eyes of hope and optimism rather than cynicism. Agape thinks about people the way God thinks about us. Love makes us think the best and believe the best about others. When we believe the worst, jump to conclusions, judge people without knowing the facts, gossip (and call it "concern"), we're not acting in love. We witness judgmental attacks in the news and social media. People are often accused and destroyed on the basis of gossip and lies (now called "misinformation" or "disinformation") without any evidence. A sinful world thrives on destroying people. That's why we need the salvation of Christ so His love fills our hearts and homes.

Agape defends people; it doesn't destroy them. Love reserves final judgment based on the facts. Love tips the scale to the side of mercy rather than judgment. "Mercy triumphs over judgment!" (James 2:13). God is slow to judge, but He "delight[s] to show mercy" (Micah 7:18). The godly fruit of love stands in contrast to the hatred, discord, jealousy, fits of rage, and selfish ambition produced by the flesh. It's sad to see even Christians divided over political, social, and cultural issues and acting out the works of the flesh instead of producing the fruit of the Spirit.

Christians are called by Christ to crucify the flesh and to cultivate the fruit. "Those who belong to Christ Jesus have crucified the sinful nature with its passions and desires. Since we live by the Spirit, let us keep in step with the Spirit" (Galatians 5:24-25). The climate of the culture is the opposite of love; it's the works of the flesh in operation. It's divisive and it's hurtful. People are slandered and ridiculed. But the fruit of love believes the best. Love is "[the] more excellent way" (1 Corinthians 12:31 NKJV).

Jesus puts His church in the midst of the culture to be His light of love to the world. We cannot act like the world if we expect to be used by the Lord to redeem the world through the gospel of Christ. Christians must act like Christ to impact the world. We have to be different in order to make a difference. Jesus changed the world because He loved people unconditionally. His love went all the way to the cross. His love is so radical that He tells us to love our enemies! When we think, feel, and act in love, we will believe the best, we will think the best, and we will act in the best interests of others.

Live the Best

Compassion takes action! Action is more important than feeling or thought. What we feel and think means nothing until we take action. Agape moves us to respond to human need. The Apostle John wrote, "If anyone has material possessions and sees his brother in need but has no pity on him, how can the love of God be in him? Dear children, let us not love with words or tongue but with actions and in truth" (1 John 3:17-18). True love is more than simply saying, "I love you." Agape is love in action.

Jesus was teaching one day to a large crowd of over 5,000 people. As evening approached, the disciples urged Him to send the crowds away so they could go to town and get something to eat. His response shocked them: "You give them something to eat" (Matthew 14:16). They went out and found a boy with his small lunch, which led to the miracle of feeding the multitude. Sometimes we want to send people away so they can fend for themselves. But Jesus tells us to help people who are in need. We must not just pray for people and send them away. If we will help them, Jesus will add His power to what we do and multiply it. We must give them something!

Agape love always helps people in need. Sometimes that means helping them economically. Sometimes it's a listening ear and a word of encouragement. Sometimes it's taking time to pray with someone, knowing that "the prayer of a righteous man is powerful and effective" (James 5:16). The Good Samaritan was willing to be inconvenienced the day he stopped to rescue the man who had been assaulted. Unlike the priest and the Levite who only saw the wounded man, he did something about what he saw. Even though it may be inconvenient, true love goes out of its way to help those in need.

Daily Commitment

Agape is a gift from God. It's only possible because of the Holy Spirit indwelling those who have been born again. If you're not born again, you can be by receiving

Christ as your Savior today. The Holy Spirit will live within you to produce the fruit of love on the tree of your life.

When you act in the flesh, be honest and recognize it. Crucify the flesh right there and tell yourself you aren't going to feel, think, or act in unloving ways. You have to denounce the flesh if you want to develop the fruit. The flesh will pull you down, but the Spirit will lift you up!

Make the commitment: I'm going to always act in love. I'm going to be moved with compassion. I'm going to believe the best, think the best, speak the best of others, and act the best toward others. I'm going to defend them, and protect them; I'm not going to destroy them. I'm going to help and never hurt others. I'm going to do something about what I see, like the Good Samaritan.

The fruit of the Spirit is love. It's true—all you need is love. You have the ability, as a child of God, to act in love. Start by identifying areas in your life where you're not acting in love. The words you say, the social media you post, the anger you feel—whatever is contrary to love, commit to stop doing it. Prayer will change you. When you pray about faulty areas in your life and ask God to help you grow up in Christ, a dramatic change will happen in you.

When we pray about our spiritual progress, we can conquer the flesh and bear good fruit. Honesty is the best policy. If we deny our faults, we won't develop the fruit.

When you see people in need, allow your heart to be moved with compassion to take action. You can change the way you think about others. Maybe you have been taught to think of people with stereotypes or biases. You can be transformed by the renewing of your mind to think of others as equals. Love will change the way you talk about others and the way you treat them. After all, we act the way we act because we think the way we think.

Racism is a great problem today. It's an unbiblical and ungodly way of thinking about people. Racism sees people as being different instead of being the same and created in God's image. Pride also is a problem. Pride looks down on others, holds prejudices, and discriminates. Love is humble and gracious and treats all people equally. Racism, pride, and prejudice are wrong ways of thinking about people. When we think right, we treat people right.

Relationships are ruined by division and jealousy. Angry outbursts come so easily when we are frustrated. So, let's "follow the way of love" (1 Corinthians 14:1). When Paul cautions us about works of the flesh (sinful nature), he says, "I warn you, as I did before, that those who live like this will not inherit the kingdom of God" (Galatians 5:21). We cannot live the Kingdom life of righteousness, peace, and joy and experience the full blessings of God if we act according to the dictates of the sinful nature. The blessed life comes when we walk in the Spirit and bear the fruit of the Spirit in every area of life.

Jesus said, "A new command I give you: Love one another. As I have loved you, so you must love one another. By this all men will know that you are my disciples, if you love one another" (John 13:34-35). Love is the only way you can prove you are a disciple of Jesus. You can change your world—your marriage, your relationship with your kids, your relationship with your family and friends, your work relationships, your relationships at church—by feeling, thinking, and acting in love.

Daily make a commitment to "put off your old self, which is being corrupted by its deceitful desires; to be made new in the attitude of your minds; and to put on the new self, created to be like God in true righteousness and holiness" (Ephesians 4:22-24). The old self consists of the works of the flesh. The new self is the fruit of the Spirit. The choice is yours. Choose to love, and you will live your best life!

2
PUT ON A HAPPY FACE

The philosopher Nietzsche said, "Christians will have to look more redeemed before I will believe their claims." We need to put on a happy face and live in a spirit of praise. As Americans, we believe in the God-given rights to life, liberty, and the pursuit of happiness.

My favorite emoji on my smartphone is the happy face. I put it on most of my text messages just to spread a little joy. The happy face makes me smile every time I see it. True happiness is one of the great marks of a true Christian. Our faith produces real joy. The birth of Jesus our Savior was an announcement of joy. The angels said to the shepherds in the field, "I bring you good news that will bring great joy to all people. The Savior—yes, the Messiah, the Lord—has been born today!" (Luke 2:10-11 NLT).

When we are born again, through faith in Jesus, a mysterious work of grace happens. God supernaturally changes the spiritual condition of our hearts. We're free from the dominance of sin, which is a destructive force. We're made righteous. We're right with God. We're made alive with Christ. We are no longer "dead in [our] transgressions and sins" (Ephesians 2:1). We're spiritually alive. We're mindful of God's presence. We live for God's glory. We find joy in helping others. These are amazing spiritual changes in our lives.

As Christians, we are born again. That means we start off as spiritual infants. All babies need to grow. Just like a healthy baby is always growing, so is a healthy Christian. As we grow spiritually, we become more like Jesus. We grow in His grace and His knowledge. Spiritual growth means we produce the fruit of joy. Fruit is not produced for the benefit of the tree but rather for those who enjoy the fruit the tree produces. When we experience joy, it benefits everyone around us.

Jesus delivers us from the works of the flesh, which are destructive. While we have the capacity to act according to the flesh, it is not the dominating force in our lives. We all struggle with the works of the flesh. When we do, we have the grace to correct our behavior because Christ lives in us. Farmers must nurture a tree for it to produce fruit. Farmers look for fruit, which means results for their work. The Holy Spirit works in our hearts so we produce spiritual fruit. The goal of spiritual growth is bearing fruit. Jesus said, "This is to my Father's glory, that you bear much fruit, showing yourselves to be my disciples" (John 15:8).

Tap the Source

The word for *joy* comes from the root word *charis*, which means "grace." Joy comes from the grace of God. Joy is a feeling of gladness, happiness, excitement, and pleasure about the state of our life. Joy is also spiritual meaning and satisfaction that comes from our relationship with Jesus, who said, "I have told you this so that my joy may be in you and that your joy may be complete" (John 15:11).

Joy is a positive outlook on life. You're confident that God is with you and He will provide for you. Joy comes from the presence of the Lord. You live in the awareness that God is with you all the time. Joy puts you in a positive mood and makes you optimistic about the future. Joy is an amazing fruit of the Holy Spirit's work in you. Remember, "It is God who works in you" (Philippians 2:13). He works in you as the greatest psychiatrist to give you joy. When you're born again, you have a new nature of joy. You can tap into that spiritual well of joy.

Joy comes from two main sources. There's situational joy and spiritual joy. Situational joy comes from life situations. Good things around us create joy within us. When people try to be hyper-spiritual and tell you joy doesn't come from circumstances, that's not true. You know better than that. If you get a promotion at work, you're joyful. But if you get fired from your job, you're disappointed. Situational joy comes from enjoying good things and experiencing good times. When things work out the way we planned, we're happy. Joy comes from our experiences. Good times create good feelings. However, when the situation changes for the worse, the joy goes away. That's because the situation is the source of the joy.

The greatest joy is spiritual, not situational. Lasting joy comes from your faith in God and experiencing His promises and presence. The joy of the Lord remains constant when the situations of life change. It is a joy derived from the Spirit of God in you, not from the situation around you. When you experience spiritual joy from the Holy Spirit, you experience contentment and peace even in the worst circumstances. While you may not be as happy as you were when things were great, you still have an incredible sense of joy because of God's presence, His faithfulness, and His unfailing love for you.

Strength for Stress

Spiritual joy is more powerful than stress. It's stronger than personal problems, negative news, or adverse conditions. Joy gives strength to handle the stress! "The joy of the Lord is your strength" (Nehemiah 8:10). Spiritual joy enabled the Apostle Paul to sit in prison with an unjust sentence and have the audacity to write, "Rejoice in the Lord always. I will say it again: Rejoice!" (Philippians 4:4). He was in a difficult situation, yet he had real joy. He tells us when we face the worst situation, we still need to rejoice.

Joy comes from rejoicing. The action creates the emotion. Joy is active, so rejoice! When you speak and act joyfully, the Holy Spirit will flood your heart with new joy. "The disciples were filled with joy and with the Holy Spirit" (Acts 13:52). When you worry, doubt, and complain, you destroy your own joy. You may not be joyful about your situation, but you can rejoice in your salvation. You aren't joyful about your problems, but you can rejoice in God's promises. You can't be joyful about your fears, but you can rejoice in your faith. You aren't joyful about your dilemma, but you can rejoice in your deliverance. Be joyful in the hope that you're going to get out of the problem and not stay stuck in it.

Spiritual joy comes from the presence, promises, and power of God. Joy is more powerful than any difficult circumstance in life. Spiritual joy is the quality of the kingdom of God. "The kingdom of God is . . . righteousness, peace and joy in the Holy Spirit" (Romans 14:17). You are in the kingdom of God and the King lives in you! "Greater is he that is in you, than he that is in the world" (1 John 4:4 KJV).

Spiritual joy comes from trusting God fully and unconditionally. "May the God of hope fill you with all joy and peace as you trust in Him, so that you may overflow with hope by the power of the Holy Spirit" (Romans 15:13). Joy comes as you *trust* in Him. Increase your trust level, and your joy level will rise! Jesus was "full of joy through the Holy Spirit" (Luke 10:21). The fruit of the Spirit is spiritual joy that cannot be defeated by problems in our personal lives or in the world around us. Joy is God's spiritual vaccine against the pressures and problems of the world.

Keep Your Joy

Spiritual joy can be lost. King David prayed, "Restore to me the joy of your salvation" (Psalm 51:12). He needed his joy restored because he lost it. The Apostle Paul asked a poignant question: "What has happened to all your joy?" (Galatians 4:15). How do we get our joy back and keep it? We can't keep situational joy because situations change, but we can keep spiritual joy because it's based on the unchanging God. "I the Lord do not change" (Malachi 3:6). Emotional feelings come and go, but the eternal facts of God's Word remain. "Now these three remain: faith, hope and love" (1 Corinthians 13:13).

While the world changes around you and emotions fluctuate within you, you can keep your joy. When you're discouraged or depressed, the joy of the Lord can deliver you. Joy is the cure for grief, disappointment, and hurt. Spiritual joy is the ultimate cure for depression.

Depression is the leading mental health problem. More people seek counseling for anxiety and depression than any other problem. While there are many effective steps to managing anxiety and depression, the greatest cure is the joy of the Lord, which is our strength.

Problems, Pressures, and People

We lose our joy for three main reasons—problems, pressures, and people. Life's problems are a joy killer. We face problems nationally, globally, and personally. Personal problems are the biggest threat to our joy and happiness. Problems such as job loss, a troubled marriage, family stress, financial insecurity, and health issues diminish our joy. When we are kids or teenagers, even problems like a poor test grade, criticism by peers, or a romantic breakup can destroy our joy.

Joy is based on your perspective. A joyful person knows problems can be solved. Joy and hope go together. Joy believes all things are possible! Life is like mathematics, in that it's all about solving problems. Mathematics is based on the premise that when we work the problem by following the formula, the problem will be solved. The laws of math work and so do the laws of life.

Joy is not just a way of feeling; it's also a way of thinking. You choose to be negative or positive. If you think positively, then you'll speak positively. The way you think and speak creates emotions. That's why you need to rejoice in both good times and bad times. You must express your joy in order to experience joy. You will experience inwardly what you express outwardly. When you rejoice, you create joy, and you will feel happier when you rejoice.

Watch out for problems. You're not going to drown in problems like the waves of the sea, for the promises of God are your life preserver. You're not going to sink and drown. Don't allow problems to eclipse your optimism and make you feel like things are never going to change or work out. Such negative thinking will make you lose your joy. You've got to tell yourself: *I'm going to get through this because I can do all things through Christ who strengthens me. I can work the problem and solve it as God gives me wisdom.* Joyful living starts with positive thinking and praiseful speaking. "We . . . believe and therefore speak" (2 Corinthians 4:13). Speak what you believe!

We lose our joy when we're under too much pressure. We often face too many demands on our time, energy, and money, and we feel the pressure. We need to live a balanced life.

Avoid overworking, poor time-management, and conflict-filled relationships. External pressure causes internal stress. *Stress* means a state of mental, emotional, and physical tension. Limit your intake of news and social media because it's often negative. Negative news steals joy and creates anxiety. Manage the stress in your life. Make sure you get plenty of regular physical exercise. Get outside the house every day and enjoy nature. Eat clean and lean meals. Spend time with your friends and family. Enjoy hobbies and take time off from work. Go to church on Sundays and get recharged! Read the Bible and talk to God. If you do, you will lower your stress and increase your joy.

People can steal your joy. Relationships enrich us and exhaust us. Some relationships fill us up while others drain us dry. Stay out of codependent relationships. You don't have to save the world. Trust me, the overly dependent can get along without you. If you are a caretaker, turn people over to God. If you're too needy, learn to trust God and stand on your own two feet. If you like the feeling of being needed, then stop rescuing people and give them space to figure life out on their own just like you did. When people need us, it feeds our sense of purpose, but that can also get us trapped in codependency.

Protect yourself in relationships. Set boundaries and don't allow yourself to be abused, neglected, or taken for granted. Hang out with people who build you up, not tear you down. You've got to love some people from a distance! Don't get entangled in unhealthy relationships. Don't blame others for the bad relationships you may be in. Get out of them. It's up to you to set boundaries and take care of yourself. If you draw the line, people will eventually respect the boundaries you set.

Consider Paul's question, "What has happened to all your joy?" We must be on guard against problems, pressures, and people to guard our joy. Do what you need to do to manage problems, lower stress, and set boundaries in your relationships. If you do, you will keep your joy!

Increase Your Joy

Since the fruit of the Spirit is joy, we need to learn how to grow the fruit. If your joy level is low, you can get it back and increase your joy. You can learn how to get more joy out of life. Joy is a powerful source of emotional, spiritual, and physical healing. "A cheerful heart is good medicine, but a crushed spirit dries up the bones" (Proverbs 17:22). Joy heals your attitude, emotions, and relationships. Joy generates energy to reach our goals. "The joy of the Lord is your strength" (Nehemiah 8:10).

Focus on the gift of salvation. Think often of God's saving grace in your life. I often rehearse in my mind the time I accepted Jesus as my Savior. I was only eight years old when I gave my heart to Christ and have never looked back from following Him. Jesus is the joy of my life. Jesus said, "These things I have spoken to you, that My joy may remain in you, and that your joy may be full" (John 15:11 NKJV). Jesus' joy is in me because He is my Savior and Lord. I pray you too may experience His joy in your heart.

A young pastor came to speak at our church. He was also an illusionist. He held our undivided attention with his tricks and his message about Jesus. I was the only person to respond to the altar call that night. He sat with me on the front row after the service concluded. Opening his Bible to John 3:16, he read the living words of Jesus: "For God so loved the world, that he gave his only begotten Son" (KJV). He then put my name in the passage as he read, "that if David would believe in Him, David would have everlasting life." He asked me, "Do you believe this promise?"

I said, "Yes, I do." Then he led me in a prayer of faith, and I trusted Christ as my Savior. I still trust Him as my Savior and believe His promise of eternal life. Jesus is the greatest source of my joy, and He can be yours as well.

When King David fell from grace, he confessed his sin and prayed, "Restore to me the joy of your salvation" (Psalm 51:12). God can restore our joy! Notice David said it is the joy of *God's salvation*. Eternal life is God's gift to us. It's not our salvation; it's His salvation given to us. When we experience His salvation, we will have joy.

You can live every day knowing you are a child of God, with the promise of everlasting life. Remember that in spite of your mistakes, God's unfailing love holds fast to the end of this life through all eternity. You are saved and kept by the grace of God. He "is able to keep you from falling and to present you before his glorious presence without fault and with great joy" (Jude 24).

Live in grace. The religious leaders in Jesus' day strike me as being very unhappy people. They were so trapped in tradition that they were joyless. They were always asking Jesus about the Law, but He would tell them about love. When we get caught up in religious traditions, rituals, and regulations, we lose our joy. We focus on our failures instead of God's faithfulness. We focus on our performance instead of God's power. We worry about our problems instead of trusting God's promises.

The Apostle Paul plainly told the Galatians they had lost their joy because they were trapped in tradition. "It is for freedom that Christ has set us free. Stand firm, then, and do not let yourselves be burdened again by a yoke of slavery" (Galatians 5:1). The "yoke of slavery" is *legalism*—trying to earn our salvation by religious customs, rules, and traditions rather than trusting the grace of God. You have to live in grace to keep your joy.

We're Saved by Grace

You're saved and kept by God's grace. Many people think they're saved by grace but kept by works. They perform religious acts to keep themselves saved as if they could lose their salvation for the slightest reason. Joy comes from knowing you're saved by grace through faith in Christ and nothing else. The words of a classic Christian hymn say, "Nothing in my hand I bring, simply to Your cross I cling."

You can't add your works to God's grace. His grace is sufficient! Our works for Christ don't make us more saved. We work in ministry because we love the Lord, not to make Heaven more guaranteed. Good works don't make you more saved. You're either saved or you're not. Salvation is purely God's work in us, not our work for Him. "Not by works, so that no one can boast" (Ephesians 2:9). It's "not by works of righteousness which we have done, but according to His mercy He saved us" (Titus 3:5 NKJV). Live by faith in the sufficiency of God's grace and you will experience joy unspeakable and full of glory.

See the Upside

Keep up your optimism. Look for the upside in everything. Control the way you think. Joy is based on controlling your thinking by a positive outlook on life. You are "transformed by the renewing of your mind" (Romans 12:2). You can transform yourself from depression to joy by renewing your mind. Depression can be biological, situational, and mental. We treat the biological aspect with proper diet and medication. We treat the situational aspect by lowering the stress factors. We control the mental aspect by a joyful outlook. Joy is an attitude— thinking about the past, the present, and the future positively. If you keep telling yourself negative messages, you will stay depressed. If you tell yourself things aren't going to get better, things aren't ever going to work out for you, life is getting worse, or the world's getting worse, you will lose your joy and slip into depression and anxiety.

Tell yourself triumphant truths like these: You can get out of your problems. You can win the battle. God has not abandoned you.

The situation you face is not impossible. All things are possible to those who believe, according to Jesus (Mark 9:23). Face life with confidence. Declare daily, "I can do all things through Christ who strengthens me" (Philippians 4:13 NKJV). Optimism is the intentional decision to look at things in a positive way and to believe the best. Stop expecting the worst and believe the best. Here's the best definition of *optimism*: "Weeping may endure a for night, but joy comes in the morning" (Psalm 30:5 NKJV). Look for a bright sunrise when you're going through the darkest night. The sun always comes up!

Optimistic people know that joy comes in the morning! It may be night right now, but sunrise is on the way! Today you may feel sad, disappointed, and anxious, but tomorrow is just around the corner. The sun is coming up and with it a fresh start. So, make new plans, dream new dreams, and pray new prayers. When you are optimistic, looking forward in faith, you will increase your joy.

Pray it up! Real prayer increases joy. I encourage you to pray. I don't mean long, drawn-out religious prayers. Simply talk to God as your heavenly Father. The best kind of prayer and the most powerful prayer is conversational prayer where you practice the presence of God. When you do, you will increase your joy. Ask Him for help. Ask Him for wisdom. Tell God exactly how you feel—let all of your emotions out. That's real prayer. That's prayer that brings the healing power of joy. The psalmist declared, "[The Lord] is at my right hand, I will not be shaken" (Psalm 16:8).

Jesus said, "Ask and you will receive, and your joy will be complete" (John 16:24). I'm not telling you to pray *more*, or to pray *long*, but to pray *right*. Praying longer or louder doesn't increase the results. It's how you pray and why you pray that matters. It's the quality and not the quantity of prayer that makes it meaningful and powerful. Jesus assures us if we ask, we will receive and our joy will be full and overflowing.

Dare to believe. Doubters aren't joyful people. Skepticism and unbelief breed depression, hopelessness, and anxiety. Faith creates joy. Simon Peter spoke of the incredible privilege he and the other disciples enjoyed by being with Jesus and witnessing His miracles and teachings firsthand. "We were eyewitnesses of his majesty" (2 Peter 1:16). He knew most believers would never have the privilege of seeing Jesus physically. But he said, "Though you have not seen him, you love him; and even though you do not see him now, you believe in him and are filled with an inexpressible and glorious joy" (1 Peter 1:8). The King James Version translates it as "joy unspeakable and full of glory." It's a joy too great for words.

If you believe in Christ, you will experience inexpressible and glorious joy. What you believe about God, about life, and about yourself determines the level of your joy. If you believe God loves you, He works all things together for your good, and He will guide your steps, then you will have inexpressible and glorious joy. The Holy Spirit lives within you and creates a deep well of spiritual water that satisfies every longing. So, you have the power to lead a joyful life. You can overcome the enemies of joy—problems, pressures, and people. You can grow and bear more fruit of joy that will bring healing to your life and to others. You will be an incredible blessing to others as the joy within overflows to others. Joy is contagious! So, share it freely.

3
PEACE TREATY

President Harry Truman said, "Peace is not a quiet or stagnant pool but a dynamic and rushing river of constant adjustment to changing conditions and unexpected opportunities."

We all want to live in peace and to experience peace of mind. God created us to live in peace. External conflicts divide people. Internal struggles create anxiety. How can we resolve conflict, lower our anxiety, and enjoy lasting peace? Faith in Jesus Christ as our Savior will bring us the blessing of peace. Jesus said, "Peace l leave with you; my peace I give you" (John 14:27).

This is why Paul said the fruit of the Spirit is peace. The Holy Spirit gives us peace to handle the problems of life when we trust God. A tree bears fruit as a natural result of the growth happening inside the tree. The effort comes in the cultivation of the soil, the planting of the seed, and the nurturing of the tree. If the tree is healthy, it will bear fruit. The natural result of the Holy Spirit working in our hearts and minds is peace. We read the Word of God to transform our minds. We pray to experience God's presence. We worship to grow in community. The more we grow spiritually, the more peaceful we become.

The feeling of peace can be situational or spiritual. Peace comes from pleasant situations. However, as soon as those situations change, that peace is gone. There's a deeper, lasting peace that's not subject to changing circumstances—the peace of God. It's greater than temporary situational peace.

Peace is more than the absence of problems, conflict, or stress. You can be in a perfect environment but still have no peace. The absence of conflict and problems doesn't create peace. Don't get me wrong—we all prefer to have no drama and no problems. But peace derives from what is happening in our life more than it is from what's not happening.

Anxiety can occur without any present problem. Anxiety is in our heart, not our environment. The problems of life make anxiety spike and increase, but the root cause is not the problems of life but our perspective. We carry our anxiety with us in good times and bad. Anxiety will increase under stress, but it doesn't go away. The only power that can defeat our anxiety is the peace of God. Spiritual peace is more powerful than stressful problems!

The Hebrew word for "peace" is *shalom*, which means "well-being." A person at peace is well, whole, and complete. Peace is a state of calmness, tranquillity, and harmony. *Shalom* means the favor and blessings of God over our lives. The Greek word for *peace* means to "bind together." The peace of God holds us together when we feel like falling apart. It is the "peace . . . which transcends all understanding" (Philippians 4:7). When things fall apart around us, God's peace holds us together. When we don't have peace, we separate, fragment, and come apart at the seams.

Jesus told Martha, "You are worried and upset about many things" (Luke 10:41). She lacked peace. Jesus, the Prince of Peace, visited her home, but she was "distracted by all the preparations that had to be made" (v. 40). She was distracted instead of focusing on the most important thing—Jesus was visiting their home, and she had the opportunity to spend time with Him. Meals can wait when the Master arrives!

The urgent ruled the important. She could cook meals but couldn't control worry. Are you distracted—worried and upset about many things? Focus on the presence of Christ within you and you will have peace. "Let the peace of Christ rule in your hearts, since as members of one body you were called to peace. And be thankful" (Colossians 3:15). When we experience spiritual peace, all of life—within us and around us—comes together in harmony. Our spirit, mind, and body are in unity. Our relationships are calm, not conflictual. Our thoughts are focused, not distracted. Our feelings are stable, not out of control.

Facts of Faith

Peace comes from the right mental perspective on life. We feel as good as we think. Good thoughts create good feelings, just as negative thinking creates bad feelings. Our belief system shapes our attitudes, values, and personality. Our belief system creates our coping skills to manage stress.

An unhealthy belief system makes us vulnerable to anxiety and depression. Our beliefs can work against us instead of working for us. We get defeated from within. When we entertain thoughts of fear, we're going to feel anxious.

Your anxiety will defeat the peace the Holy Spirit gives you. If you tell yourself there's no hope, then you're going to feel hopeless. Your depression, fueled by your negative beliefs, will defeat you from within. Here are three facts of faith you need to believe to experience spiritual peace.

1. *Believe Christ has saved you.* "You shall call His name JESUS, for He will save His people from their sins" (Matthew 1:21 NKJV). Paul writes, "For it is by grace you have been saved" (Ephesians 2:8). You are saved from sin, judgment, and death and saved for abundant and eternal life! People have anxiety about their relationship with God. They doubt their salvation. Jesus tells us, "You believe in God, believe also in Me. . . . Peace I leave with you, My peace I give to you; not as the world gives. . . . Let not your heart be troubled, neither let it be afraid" (John 14:1, 27 NKJV).

You need to believe you belong to Jesus and are kept safe in this world and the next by His power. Don't doubt His presence with you or His promises to you. If you believe you have eternal life through Christ, you will be at peace.

2. *Believe God is sovereign in your life.* The word *sovereign* refers to ruling and governing. God is in control. That doesn't mean He causes everything. It simply means in everything that happens, God is in control and He decides how everything turns out. "In all things God works for the good of those who love him, who have been called

according to his purpose" (Romans 8:28). If you believe God is working in everything you experience for your good, then you will live in peace.

3. *Believe you are secure for Heaven.* Some people suffer from eternal insecurity. Jesus saved you to give you security. Eternal life is His personal promise to everyone who trusts Him. Some people know they are saved by God's grace, but they falsely believe they are kept by works. They are torn between trusting and trying. I have talked to Christians who are not sure if they will really go to Heaven. Here is God's promise: "To him who is able to keep you from falling and to present you before his glorious presence without fault and with great joy" (Jude 24). Jude, the brother of Jesus, wrote those words to give us assurance of our salvation. God is able! We aren't able to stand on our own, but God is able! He is able to keep us from falling.

When God calls you home to Heaven, He will present you to the hosts of Heaven "without fault and with great joy." You and I aren't faultless in ourselves, but we stand in the faultlessness of Christ. Pilate said of Jesus, "I find no fault in this Man" (Luke 23:4 NKJV). If we are clothed with Christ's righteousness, God will welcome us into Heaven as His own. The Apostle Peter said we will "receive a rich welcome into the eternal kingdom of our Lord and Savior Jesus Christ" (2 Peter 1:11).

A rich welcome means a grand entry with a great celebration! How awesome it is to know we will stand before God's glorious presence without fault and with great joy. We won't tremble before His glorious presence like Isaiah did when he saw the Lord highly exalted and angels declaring, "Holy, holy, holy is the Lord God Almighty."

Isaiah said, "Woe is me! . . . I am ruined!" (Isaiah 6:3, 5). We, however, will stand before God's glorious presence without fault and with great joy!

If you accept Jesus' gift of eternal life, you will have peace in this life and the life to come. "Whoever believes in Him has eternal life" (see John 3:15). If you listen to your fears, you will lose your peace. But if you listen to the promises of God's Word, you will live in peace. Peace is the fruit of faith. So, fix your broken belief system by faith in the promises of God! Life's problems bring panic, but God's promises bring peace. "For no matter how many promises God has made, they are 'Yes' in Christ" (2 Corinthians 1:20).

Matter of the Mind

Ralph Waldo Emerson said, "A person is what he or she thinks about all day long." Peace comes from how you think about life, world events, and yourself. Peace is a matter of the mind. Jesus said, "Do not let your hearts be troubled" (John 14:27). You decide whether your heart is troubled or not. You can't control the trouble in the world, but you can control the trouble in your heart. If you feed your heart bad news, negative news, fake news, and hysterical news, it will raise your anxiety level. If you feed your mind on good news, you will enjoy peace. The psalmist David said, "Great peace have they who love your law, and nothing can make them stumble" (Psalm 119:165).

The Apostle Paul described the spiritual peace he experienced, even though he was in prison, as something which "transcends all understanding" (Philippians 4:7). Then, he gave us the secret to peace—thought control:

"Whatever is true, whatever is noble, whatever is right, whatever is pure, whatever is lovely, whatever is admirable—if anything is excellent or praiseworthy—think about such things" (v. 8).

The word *think* means to dwell, to fixate, and to meditate deeply about these things. What if we lived in a world where all the news we heard was true, noble, right, pure, lovely, and admirable? We wouldn't have an epidemic of anxiety and depression. Since we don't live in a perfect world, we need to counteract negativism with positive and wholesome thoughts.

When you think right, you will have peace, knowing "the God of peace will be with you" (Philippians 4:9). Guard your heart and your mind against negative information and empty imaginations. "Above all else, guard your heart, for it is the wellspring of life" (Proverbs 4:23). Protect your mind against lies, fears, and pessimism. What goes in the mind comes back out. So, let the peace stand guard over your heart and your mind as you rest in the power, presence, and protection of God over your life and your family. When you believe the best, you will feel your best.

Peaceful Prayer

Peace comes through prayer. Prayer is a personal conversation with God based on trust. When the disciples heard Jesus praying, it sounded like He was talking directly to God. He taught us to pray, "Our Father, who is in Heaven." Jesus shows us how to pray and how not to pray. When we practice His presence all day long, we can "pray without ceasing" (1 Thessalonians 5:17 KJV). The words of the song "What a Friend We Have in Jesus" teach us about peace: "Oh, what peace we often forfeit, Oh, what needless pain we bear, All because we do not carry Everything to God in prayer!"

When I hear some people pray, it raises my anxiety level instead of lowering it. Some people use prayer to vent their emotions. Others use prayer to lecture those listening to them (they're talking to the people present instead of to God!). Prayer is not repeating mantras. Prayer is not rehearsing our anxiety; it's releasing it into the hands of God. So, when you pray, "Cast all your anxiety on [the Lord] because he cares for you" (1 Peter 5:7).

Jesus told us when we pray, not to keep repeating the same thing. "When you pray, do not keep on babbling like pagans, for they think they will be heard because of their many words. Do not be like them, for your Father knows what you need before you ask him" (Matthew 6:7-8). Release, don't repeat!

Venting our feelings is fine, and even helpful, but it's not prayer. Venting emotions can even intensify our feelings instead of relieving them. When we rehearse anger, we get angrier. When we dwell on our fears, we become more frightened. Real prayer means releasing anxiety, not rehearsing it. Release your anger, don't rehearse it. Release your guilt; don't rehearse it. Put your concerns in God's hands and trust Him to work things out, because "[He] works out everything in conformity with the purpose of his will" (Ephesians 1:11).

When you release your worry and let it go, the peace of God will guard your heart. Peace is your security system, keeping fear from breaking into your heart. "Do not be anxious about anything, but in everything, by prayer and petition, with thanksgiving, present your requests to God. And the peace of God, which transcends all understanding, will guard your hearts and your minds in Christ Jesus" (Philippians 4:6-7).

What do you do when anxiety comes back after you pray it away? Pray again! Pray the prayer of release until you believe what you're praying! Too often we offer prayers we don't fully believe. We all need to grow in our faith. The more we pray, the stronger our faith will grow. "Build yourselves up in your most holy faith and pray in the Holy Spirit" (Jude 20).

Pray through your uncertainties, doubts, and fears until you believe the unchanging promises of God. You can receive peace only if you believe in God's purpose and providence. "Everything is possible for him who believes," Jesus said (Mark 9:23). Your level of peace depends on three words: *If you believe.* When your mind tells you to worry, then declare, "I'm not going to worry. I'm going to worship because I have given the situation to God and He's working all things together for my good!"

Emotional Management

Peace comes from emotional management. Manage your emotions and they won't manipulate you. Cleanse your heart from toxic emotions. "Come near to God and he will come near to you. Wash your hands, you sinners, and purify your hearts, you double-minded" (James 4:8).

Take this challenge to heart: "Get rid of all bitterness, rage and anger, brawling and slander, along with every form of malice" (Ephesians 4:31). Emotional management starts with a clean heart as we get rid of negative emotions. Then we can "be kind and compassionate to one another, forgiving each other, just as in Christ God forgave you" (v. 32). As God's kids, we need to act like God! "Be imitators of God . . . as dearly loved children and live a life of love, just as Christ loved us and gave himself up for us as a fragrant offering and sacrifice to God" (5:1-2).

When you are at peace with God and yourself, you will be a peacemaker. When you lack peace, you cause tension and anxiety in relationships. Anxiety and anger are toxic emotions both to us and to others. So, get rid of all bitterness, rage, and anger. Such feelings are the root cause of conflict in our relationships. Don't speak or act in anger. Get rid of brawling (fighting) and slander (saying critical things of others). Get rid of "every form of malice," which means an attitude of retaliation and revenge, hoping others get what's coming to them. Instead, we should pray for the best to happen to others. Jesus said, "Love your enemies" (Luke 6:27).

The Scripture says, "Get rid of *all*." We need to clean out the emotional closet of all bitterness, anger, and rage. A couple times a year, Barbie does what she calls a deep cleaning of the house. Every day she cleans the house because both of us are clean freaks! We don't like anything unclean or cluttered or old. We like everything new, orderly, and clean. We all need deep cleaning in our hearts and minds to live at peace.

King David prayed, "Create in me a clean heart, O God" (Psalm 51:10 NKJV). When toxic feelings rise in our hearts, we need to get rid of them immediately in a moment of prayer. Stop and pray, "Father, create in me a clean heart and remove all anger and anxiety by the power of the Holy Spirit, in Jesus' powerful name!"

When we imitate God and live a life of love, we will experience the peace of God that only the Holy Spirit can give. We will never be at peace with ourselves until we are at peace with God and with others. William Hazlitt (1778-1830) said, "Those who are at war with others are not at peace with themselves."

People are saying America is more divided now than it's ever been. I'm sure that's not true because this country suffered a Civil War many years ago. Historically, that's the most divided the nation has ever been. I am not divided with anyone! I hope you're not divided. The way of Christ is the way of unity, not division. "Make every effort to keep the unity of the Spirit through the bond of peace" (Ephesians 4:3). Unity and peace go together. When we live in unity, we experience peace. When we are peaceful, we create unity. The power of God's grace gives us inner unity—spirit, mind, and body—and outward unity as we "live at peace with everyone" (Romans 12:18).

As we get rid of negative emotions, we experience three positive emotions—kindness, compassion, and forgiveness. *Kindness* means to feel empathy and to act in ways to benefit and help others rather than harm them. Kindness is seen in Jesus' parable of the good shepherd, who left 99 sheep in the fold to look for the one lost sheep. He searched until he found it. Kindness is seen in Nicodemus and Joseph of Arimathea who, at the risk of their own reputation and at their own expense, went to Pontius Pilate to request the body of Jesus to honor Him with a royal burial.

Compassion is love in action. Love motivates us to help those in need. Love is the feeling while compassion is the action. "When Jesus . . . saw a large crowd, he had compassion on them and healed their sick" (Matthew 14:14). When Jesus saw a lonely leper, He was moved with compassion to the point that He touched the leper and cured him. When the Prodigal Son returned home, his father was moved with compassion to the point that he ran out of the house to embrace his son with a kiss and throw him a party.

Saul was filled with jealous hatred toward David. For ten years, David ran from Saul's soldiers. However, David said of Saul, "May I never lift my hand against him, for he is the Lord's anointed" (see 1 Samuel 24:6). David never spoke a critical word against King Saul. David knew that judgment belongs to God, not to people. When Saul died, David sought to show kindness to Saul's family.

Forgiveness is a financial term that means to cancel the debt. If your credit card company calls you today and says they're forgiving your debt, that means you have a zero balance on your credit card. Forgiveness also means to give up a grudge, release resentment, and bless the offender. Forgiveness is also a feeling. It's a feeling that leads to action, and it's an action that leads to a feeling. When you truly forgive someone, even when you have the ability to punish them or get even, then your anger will subside and you will experience the peace of God!

Play Nice

Parents teach little children the importance of playing nice. When drama starts, parents break up kids fighting over a toy and tell them, "Kids, play nice." We have two long-haired miniature dachshunds, Mikey and Beau; and when they get tangled up, Barbie tells them, "Boys, play nice." It's a virtue we need to treasure as adults. When we get mad and fight others, God speaks in our hearts, "Play nice."

Peace comes from how well you get along with others. So, play nice. Peace is the fruit of how you treat others. If you cause conflict, you get conflict. If you pursue peace, you will get peace. So, "pursue peace with all people, and holiness, without which no one will see the Lord" (Hebrews 12:14 NKJV). People who create conflict, fight with others, and attack others disturb their own inner peace. When you trouble others, you only end up creating trouble for yourself.

My father would caution me, "David, don't bring trouble on yourself." Wisdom reminds us, "He who brings trouble on his family will inherit only wind" (Proverbs 11:29). We reap what we sow. We get a return on what we invest. We receive what we give. "Peacemakers who sow in peace raise a harvest of righteousness" (James 3:18). Sow peace and you will live in peace. Sow the seeds of peace in your words and actions and you will reap righteousness, which means things will go right for you.

Christians are ambassadors of Christ. Jesus said, "Blessed are the peacemakers, for they will be called sons of God" (Matthew 5:9). The word *blessed* means "happy." Happiness comes from making peace, not from causing trouble. When you see people fighting, help them resolve their conflict. When someone verbally attacks you, defend yourself but don't strike back. When someone attacks or criticizes you on social media, ignore it. Be a peacemaker. Be kind, compassionate, and forgiving.

While we live in an anxious and angry world, we can make a peace treaty—peace with God, peace with others, and peace within ourself. The fruit of the Spirit is peace.

4
WHEN PATIENCE COUNTS

A Chinese proverb says, "Nothing makes victory so certain as does patience." Ours is a fast-moving, impatient world. If you're like me, you struggle with patience. At times, I'm in such a hurry to get things done I don't have time for patience!

As we grow spiritually, we develop the power of patience. Hebrews 6:12 teaches believers, "We [want you] to imitate those who through faith and patience inherit what has been promised."

Since there are misconceptions about patience, let's discover its real meaning. What is patience? Why do we need it? How can we grow the spiritual fruit of patience in our lives?

The word *patience* can be translated as "long-suffering." I like that word better because it graphically describes what patience does. *Patience* means to suffer long—to put up with difficult things and wait for things to happen at the proper time. Patience involves a level of suffering. When we suffer long with people and situations, we are being patient. The Greek word *makrothumia* puts two words together. The word *makro* means "long" and *thumia* means "temper," or "emotion." So, patience means having a long fuse! Patience means to pause before we vent our feelings and frustrations. Patience means to keep a level head instead of "flying off the handle." Slow down your responses and you will improve your relationships.

Slowing down enables us to control anger. When you get mad, upset, or frustrated, slow your roll. Anger is like a wildfire. When it breaks out, it destroys everything quickly. Patience is the firewall to keep the fire contained in one room so it doesn't burn down the house. The virtue of patience enables us to control our emotions rather than letting them control us. The word *patience* is often paired with *perseverance* and *endurance* in the New Testament.

Perseverance is a form of patience and vital to reach our goals. We endure things patiently. We persevere toward our goal patiently. Time plus tenacity is true patience. Success belongs to those who stick it out, press through pain, and never quit. Here's how John the Revelator described the last days: "This calls for patient endurance and faithfulness on the part of the saints" (Revelation 13:10). "Patient endurance" is time plus tenacity.

Waiting in Line

When I was young, our family would go to a local cafeteria for Sunday after church. We sometimes had to stand in a line so long that it started in the parking lot. One hot summer Sunday we were baking in the sun wearing our Sunday best. I was hungry, restless, and complained about having to wait.

I told my mom, "When I grow up, I'm never going to wait in line at a restaurant."

She said, "Maybe so, but you're going to wait in this line!"

Technology, fast food, and online shopping condition us to be impatient. We want everything now! My pastor used to say God is not a computer operator; He's a farmer! Farming takes time. The farmer has to cultivate the soil, plant the seed, nurture the growth, and reap the harvest. Farming moves in seasons that can never be rushed. Farmers know how to wait to get a great harvest.

The world of technology has made us more impatient, but patience brings great benefits. Success comes from patience. Healthy relationships require patience. Marriage and parenting thrive on patience. Think about the mistakes we make when we act impatiently. We have to apologize for what we said and try to undo the damage. Fixing the damage is more work than slowing down our frustration, holding our tongue, and restraining our actions.

Impatience gets us in trouble. "Better a patient man than a warrior, a man who controls his temper than one who takes a city" (Proverbs 16:32). It's normal to get impatient sitting in traffic, being put on hold on the phone, standing in a long line, or waiting for guests to leave when they've overstayed their welcome. If you're not impatient in those times, there's something wrong with you!

We need to value the power of patience. We need to slow our roll and not overreact when we feel impatient.

When we get impatient and irritated, we should tell our-self, "Slow down! Calm down! Don't say it. Don't do any-thing. Wait!" Patience gives us mastery over emotions so we don't overreact.

Act Like God

Patience and *perseverance* are different. Patience re-lates to people, while perseverance relates to projects. Persevere in your work. Persevere in athletics and exer-cise. Persevere toward your goals. Patience means being gentle and understanding with people. Patience is vital to healthy relationships. Be patient in your marriage and patient with your kids. Be patient with your friends. Be patient with the people and the pastor of your church. Churches aren't perfect. They're made up of imperfect people, so "clothe yourselves with compassion" (Colos-sians 3:12) toward one another. "Be patient, bearing with one another in love" (Ephesians 4:2).

Think about how patient God is with us. He is a long-suffering God. He is merciful and overlooks our faults. When we are patient, we imitate God. That's what it means to be godly. Jesus told a parable about forgiving a person who sins against you seventy times seven for the same offense! He was teaching us to forgive others an un-limited number of times. Forgive and keep on forgiving. That's patience! We need to go the extra mile and give people a second chance, and a third chance if they need it. Remembering how patient God is with us helps us to be patient with others.

I avoid long lines. However, many situations require us to be patient. Difficult circumstances don't change overnight. Problems aren't solved overnight. Goals aren't reached overnight. When we get impatient with situations and quit, we fall short of success. Impatience causes people to give up on their goals because things aren't moving as fast as they expected.

Don't stop short of reaching goals, fulfilling dreams, and achieving ambitions. When it comes to people, projects, and problems, be patient. Give it time. Great accomplishments take longer than you think they will take. So, stay the course. Face setbacks with confidence. Setbacks can't stop you if you stay patient and see things through the end. Patience yields the fruit of success, reward, and achievement. Remember, God is patient with you. Show the same patience with the important people in your life. Let go of unrealistic expectations. Give people room for failure. Jesus said, "By your patience possess your souls" (Luke 21:19 NKJV).

Patient Plans

God's plan unfolds gradually, so be patient as He fulfills His purpose for you. God will give you a dream and vision for your life, but that doesn't mean it's going to happen right now. Faith means waiting on God. Waiting is the answer to worry. If you will wait on God in faith, you won't worry so much. When you pray about an issue, don't get disappointed if the answer doesn't come immediately or things don't change instantly.

God works in His perfect time. "There is a time for everything, and a season for every activity under heaven" (Ecclesiastes 3:1). God told the prophet Habakkuk about the vision He gave him: "Though it linger, wait for it; it will certainly come" (Habakkuk 2:3). When God gives you a vision, He will bring it to pass in His time. Trust God's time. If you're patient, you'll see it come to pass. If you're patient, you'll see your prayers fulfilled in God's time and in His way. If you're patient, you'll see His purpose fulfilled and His plan accomplished. "So do not throw away your confidence; it will be richly rewarded. You need to persevere so that when you have done the will of God, you will receive what he has promised" (Hebrews 10:35-36).

Patience means long-suffering. You need to suffer long with people and with projects. You need to endure to the end if you want to succeed. The only real failure in life is when you stop trying. Endure the process of your goals with joy. "Consider it pure joy . . . whenever you face trials of many kinds" (James 1:2). Patience does not mean grinding it out with a bad attitude. Patience is a positive attitude of confidence. You will succeed if you wait.

Patience is joyful and optimistic. When you truly believe you will reach the goal, you will wait for it patiently. Faith and patience go hand in hand. Since you know God is faithful, wait on Him. "If we hope for what we do not yet have, we wait for it patiently. In the same way, the Spirit helps us in our weakness" (Romans 8:25-26). The Holy Spirit will help you overcome your impatience as you wait in faith for the promises and purpose of God.

Patience Plus

Since patience is the fruit of the Spirit, how can you produce more of it? When you are impatient, pause and pray for the Holy Spirit to calm you down. Trust God's timing in everything you pray about and everything you are working toward. Remember, "He has made everything beautiful in its time" (Ecclesiastes 3:11). Trust His time, not your time. Trusting God includes trusting His timeframe.

The Holy Spirit helps us with the weakness of impatience. Prayer is depending on the Holy Spirit in your weaknesses, whatever they are. Patience begins with yielding to the Holy Spirit in prayer. Jesus told the disciples, "I will ask the Father, and he will give you another Counselor to be with you forever—the Spirit of truth" (John 14:16-17). The word *counselor* means "one summoned to help."

Ask the Holy Spirit to fill you with power and grace. "Be filled with the Spirit" (Ephesians 5:18). When you are impatient, irritated, and frustrated, pause and pray: *Lord, fill me with the Spirit and give me the power of patience. Anoint me with power to walk in patience as I deal with tough problems, work with difficult people, and pursue Your plan. Lord, I trust Your perfect timing.* Patience comes from focused prayer and dependency on the Holy Spirit.

Patience also comes by problems. You're not going to like this and neither do I, but trials, tests, and troubles help develop our level of patience.

> Consider it pure joy . . . whenever you face trials of many kinds, because you know that the testing of your faith develops perseverance. . . . Blessed is the man who perseveres under trial, because when he has stood the test, he will receive the crown of life that God has promised to those who love him (James 1:2-3, 12).

Life's trials provide the laboratory to develop patience. You can't grow without some grief in your life. When you face problems, ask yourself what you can learn from the experience. Don't waste your problems. Get better, not bitter. Trials will help transform you if you take advantage of them.

Patience is learned through failure, which is painful but effective. Failure is very educational. Damage control is hard work when we make a mess of things. It takes more work to fix the damage caused by impatience than it does to be patient. When we take time with people and projects, we learn to value the peace that comes with patience. We regret the times we spoke harshly or acted rashly. We have to clean up the mess we caused by getting in a hurry. Such mistakes teach us patience.

Impatience is a great teacher. Impatience punishes us for our immaturity and insensitivity. The failure of impatience teaches us the importance of patience. We may learn the hard way, but at least we learn!

Patience rewards us. When we are patient, hold our tongue, slow our pace, and maintain our composure, we succeed in life and in our relationships. We all regret the times we sent a text message or email rashly in anger, when we should have hit DELETE instead of sending it. On the other hand, when we show patience to someone and overlook mistakes, we feel good about ourselves. That's when we act like Jesus.

The positive feeling that comes from being patient rewards us for our good behavior. Human behavior is conditioned by rewards. The rewards of patience help us grow in Christ-like character.

Let's endeavor to show more patience. It's one of the best-kept secrets to success.

5
KILL THEM WITH KINDNESS

The phrase "kill them with kindness" means to surprise someone by treating them in a way that is extremely kind or helpful. Instead of returning an insult, try killing them with kindness. Jesus said, "If someone strikes you on one cheek, turn to him the other also" (Luke 6:29).

When Pontius Pilate asked Jesus where His kingdom was located, He replied, "My kingdom is not of this world" (John 18:36). So, where does the kingdom of God come from and what kind of kingdom is it? Jesus said His kingdom does not come with observation because "the kingdom of God is within you" (Luke 17:20-21).

When you are born again by faith in Jesus, a Kingdom transfer takes place in your life. "For he [God] has rescued us from the dominion of darkness and brought us into the kingdom of the Son he loves" (Colossians 1:13). The kingdom of God is diametrically opposed to the kingdoms of this world. You change citizenship from earth to Heaven! Now, your "citizenship is in heaven" (Philippians 3:20).

The devil offered Jesus the kingdoms of this world and their splendor if the Son of God would bow down and worship him. Jesus refused the devil's offer because His kingdom is far greater than the kingdoms of this world. The kingdom of God is a realm of kindness. The kingdoms of this world function by competition, strife, and division. The world system takes revenge, advocates payback, and harbors grudges.

The kingdom of God, however, is marked by kindness. The character within us shapes the world around us. The Holy Spirit lives within us from the moment we accept Jesus as our Savior. The Spirit of God changes our character, temperament, mood, and personality, so that we reflect the character of Jesus. The fruit of the Spirit are nine qualities of a Christ-like person. Bearing spiritual fruit means the same thing as being conformed to the image of Christ. As citizens of Heaven, we live under the government of the living God, who is kind and merciful. Since we are God's children, we naturally treat others with kindness just like our heavenly Father treats us.

As the fruit of kindness grows in our heart, it enriches our relationships. We are better people when we are kind, and people are better off when we are kind to them. The Greek word for *kindness* is *chrestotes*, meaning something is "sweet, pleasant, useful, and excellent." Kindness means being pleasant, easy to get along with, and not fighting or being contentious. It is living an excellent life and treating others with the highest standard of care. Kindness means to be useful and beneficial and never harmful. "Love does no harm to its neighbor. Therefore, love is the fulfillment of the law" (Romans 13:10).

KILL THEM WITH KINDNESS

The ancient Greeks used the word *kindness* to mean showing interest in other people instead of being self-absorbed. One Bible scholar noted kindness means looking outward instead of looking inward. It's easy to be self-centered, always looking inward. Kindness is looking to serve the interests of others. The Apostle Paul challenged believers, "Each of you should look not only to your own interests, but also to the interests of others" (Philippians 2:4).

We're living in a day when people shout down opposing views. Adults act like kids having a temper tantrum. Kindness respects the right for people to express their views even though it's not our view. We don't have to respect their view, but we respect their right to have it.

Kindness means showing mutual respect. Jesus said, "My yoke is easy and my burden is light" (Matthew 11:30). The word *easy* in this passage is the Greek word *chrestotes*. So Jesus is saying, "My yoke is kindness." Kindness makes things easy, not difficult. When we are kind, we are easygoing—easy to get along with and easy to talk with.

The Word of God gives us three powerful ways to show kindness—the words we speak, the way we feel, and the way we act:

> Do not let any unwholesome talk come out of your mouths, but only what is helpful for building others up according to their needs, that it may benefit those who listen. And do not grieve the Holy Spirit of God, with whom you were sealed for the day of redemption. Get rid of all bitterness, rage and anger, brawling and slander, along with every form of malice. Be kind and compassionate to one another, forgiving each other, just as in Christ God forgave you (Ephesians 4:29-32).

Love Talk

Kindness is shown in the way we speak to others; we must not let "unwholesome talk," or "corrupt communication" (v. 29 KJV) come out of our mouth. *Unwholesome* means something that contaminates and causes deterioration (like termites, mold, or acid).

Our speech should be *wholesome*. The easiest way to be kind is to guard the way we talk to others. This includes texting, emails, and social media. Words may not be coming out of our mouths, per se, but they're coming out of our fingertips. Kindness starts with eliminating unkind words. When you have an unkind thought, don't say it; instead, keep it in your mind. Resolve your feelings privately in prayer or talk with someone confidentially.

The word *unwholesome* in Greek (*sapros*) means "rotten." If you mix rotten fruit with good fruit, the good will be ruined. Deterioration spreads and ruins good fruit. Unhealthy and unkind words ruin our relationships. Unwholesome talk ruins family relationships, business deals, political progress, and church unity. Unwholesome talk ruins the media, news, movies, music, and education. Young people are being taught in schools to discriminate and to label themselves as either oppressors or victims. Such negative labels spoken to young people is a form of unwholesome talk that divides and destroys. That's the way the world talks, but as God's people we speak a higher language—the words of faith, hope, and love. Our speech is seasoned with grace so we build others up instead of tearing them down.

Positive and powerful speech "is helpful for building others up according to their needs, that it may benefit those who listen" (v. 29). Good communication uses words that are helpful and never hurtful so we can benefit others. This includes the way we speak *to* people and the way we speak *about* people. Godly words build up, not tear down. When you put the needs of others ahead of your own, you will guard your speech. While you may want to vent your anger, people don't need to hear it.

We should never criticize the church. Instead, "[let everything] be done for the strengthening of the church" (1 Corinthians 14:26). We are called to strengthen the church, not weaken it. We build up the church by constructive speech. Christians and churches are all imperfect. We must never harm the church, for whom Christ died. "Christ loved the church and gave himself up for her" (Ephesians 5:25).

The world persecutes us and criticizes us. We counterattack such attacks by building ourselves up in our "most holy faith" (Jude 20). Always speak well of the church, which is the object of Jesus' love as His bride. God will bless you as you bless His church.

What's true of national Israel is also true of Christ's church. God told Abraham, "I will bless those who bless you, and whoever curses you I will curse; and all peoples on earth will be blessed through you" (Genesis 12:3). Christians are grafted into the tree of Israel (Romans 11:19). Believers in Christ are heirs of the covenant. "If you belong to Christ, then you are Abraham's seed, and heirs according to the promise" (Galatians 3:29). Paul called the church "the Israel of God" (6:16). When we bless the church of Christ, we will be blessed.

Wholesome talk benefits those who listen. Those who listen includes the people we talk to directly and the people they are going to tell! There are no secrets! Early in my ministry I used to tell leaders that our meetings were confidential. I no longer do that because it's implied by the nature of a meeting and creating a culture of confidentiality. I learned if you have to ask for confidentiality, you have the wrong leaders. The fact is, in most cases, if you say something, it's going to get repeated. We need to be careful in choosing our words because confidentiality is a lost virtue. The Greek word used here for *benefit* literally means to administer grace to someone. The word *benefit* comes from the word *grace*. When we show kindness and speak kindly, we impart God's grace. Grace means blessing and favor that we speak and show to others.

When we get a new job, we look carefully at the company's employee benefits package. Our words should always benefit people. The Greek word for *benefit* is our word *eulogy*. It simply means to speak well of someone and in that sense to show them grace and favor. Funeral services often include people giving the deceased a eulogy, in which they share personal memories to honor their loved ones. Our words should benefit and minister grace. We need to give our friends and family their eulogy on this side of Heaven! Tell them today how much you love them and are grateful for them. Tell someone "Thank you" today!

We need people to eulogize us now; we don't need a eulogy when we're in Heaven. We're going to hear Jesus tell us, "Well done, good and faithful servant." So, give somebody their eulogy today. Don't wait until they've left this world before you say something great about them. Call them today. Text them today. Tell them how great they are. Bless them today. Benefit them today. Minister grace to them today. That's the easiest and quickest and most powerful way we can bear the fruit of kindness—by the words we speak.

The Old Testament tells us about a righteous man named Job who was attacked by the devil. He lost his children in a tragic storm. His wealth was stolen by thieves. Raiders attacked his farm and stole his cattle, sheep, and oxen. His wife fell into depression and experienced a crisis of faith. He became seriously ill. Then he had three friends visit him in his suffering. They sat with him for seven days and shared his grief. "They set out from their homes and met together by agreement to go and sympathize with him and comfort him. . . . They saw how great his suffering was" (Job 2:11-13).

After the seven days, "Job opened his mouth and cursed the day of his birth" (3:1). Job wished he had never been born. Who can blame him for his feelings? Eliphaz encouraged Job, telling him, "[Job,] your words have supported those who stumbled; [your words] have strengthened faltering knees" (4:4). Kindness is shown when we speak supportive words to someone who has stumbled. Unfortunately, his friends went from comfort to criticism and from sympathy to speculation, suggesting Job was to blame for all his problems. In the end, God said their spiritual conclusions on the mystery of suffering were all wrong. God told his friends (who needs friends like that?), "I am angry with you . . . because you have not spoken of me what is right, as my servant Job has" (42:7).

We need to speak kind words to help people in their suffering. Do our words support people who have stumbled? Do you know somebody who has stumbled? Your kind words will pick them up. Let's eliminate any unwholesome talk that deteriorates and choose words that are helpful for building others up according to their needs.

Feel Great

We express kindness through keeping emotional balance and expressing emotions in a healthy manner. Emotions come and go. They can shift in a split second. We can go from the greatest high point to the lowest point in an instant. Emotions are highly reactive and sometimes unpredictable. When people attack us verbally or on social media, it's easy to lash out in anger. That's when the spiritual fruit of kindness is needed. Only the Holy Spirit working in our hearts and minds can give us the power to turn the other cheek.

By God's grace, we must "get rid of all bitterness, rage and anger, brawling and slander, along with every form of malice" (Ephesians 4:31). It's like taking out the trash. As soon as the trash can is full, we get it out of the house. We don't let trash store up unless we're hoarders! Negative emotions build up like trash in our heart, and we need to get rid of them. Feelings like hurt, anger, and disappointment need to be disposed of quickly. "Do not let the sun go down while you are still angry, and do not give the devil a foothold" (vv. 26-27).

Repressed emotions cause us to be irritated and set us on edge to lash out at the first person who provokes us. Disappointment festers and causes feelings of hopelessness and powerlessness. So, take out the trash. Get things off your chest. Make things right in your relationships. Vent your feelings in prayer. Talk to a friend you trust and get rid of negative emotions.

The Apostle Paul said we must eliminate "all kinds of bitterness." Bitterness comes in many forms and is the result of unresolved, deep-seated anger. We store up angry feelings (instead of taking out our emotional trash) and then we boil over. When anger is harbored, people grow bitter. So, make a commitment now to grow better, not bitter, regardless of what happens to you. The Bible calls it a "bitter root [that] grows up to cause trouble and defile many" (Hebrews 12:15).

Aristotle defined a *bitter* person as someone with whom it is "hard to be reconciled." Once a relationship is broken, you try to reconcile with them and tell them you are sorry, but they reject the apology and the effort to be reconciled. That's why the Bible says, "If it is possible, as far as it depends on you, live at peace with everyone" (Romans 12:18). Some people don't want to live at peace. They feel justified in their anger and morally superior by venting on social media. Such people have a root of bitterness growing in their heart. When it sprouts up, the root causes trouble and defiles everyone in their sphere of influence. Bitterness spreads to others and ruins relationships, families, churches, and businesses.

Then, we need to get rid of "rage and anger." These two words together mean outbursts of anger. It's seen in road rage. Personally, I never get mad at people when driving unless they are dangerous. If somebody jumps in front of me, I figure they're a better driver. I think, *That was a good move.* There's no reason for you to get angry while driving. Give other drivers the benefit of the doubt. That's what it means to show the fruit of kindness. Choose to believe the best about others rather than assuming the worst. Maybe the other driver didn't see you or they needed to get across a few lanes to take the next exit. Maybe they're just a lousy driver! Whatever the case, get rid of road rage.

Angry outbursts are not only verbal; they can also be physical. Get rid of the bad habit of angry outbursts. Learn to practice emotional restraint. Take a deep breath, get centered, and stay calm. When you do, the fruit of kindness will blossom in its place.

We also need to get rid of "brawling and slander." The Greek word for *brawling* means "shouting and speaking abusively." People shout in protest, arguments, and debate. We shout people down because we don't want to listen to their perspective, experience, or feelings. People shout at each other with words, text messages, and social-media posts. However, the more you shout, the less people respect you and the less effective you are in communication.

The word *slander* means "blasphemy" and "gossip." Gossip isn't merely lying about somebody and bearing false witness. It also includes breaking a sacred trust by sharing confidential information. It's not about whether the information is true or false, but whether or not it hurts the person. It doesn't matter what you know about them. It's not your place to share the information unless it is required for someone else's safety and well-being. "Love covers over a multitude of sins" (1 Peter 4:8). Don't expose people through gossip. Instead, cover them with love and keep their problems a secret.

Love covers, but anger gossips. Gossip comes from jealousy and anger. We're mad at somebody. We want to see them get what's coming to them. That's why people gossip. It never comes from a good place. People rationalize their gossip by saying, "I'm only trying to help." But that's not true. Gossip is never helpful. "A gossip betrays a confidence . . . and separates close friends" (Proverbs 11:13; 16:28). Gossip is never godly. It is never healthy. Gossip stirs up conflict, destroys confidence, and dwarfs character.

Let's get rid of slander/gossip. Let's get rid of pent-up anger, brawling, and shouting. Let's get rid of it all and live with excellence, dignity, and honor.

Finally, we are taught to get rid of *malice*, which means "inherent meanness, badness, and evil intent." People can lash out at others just to hurt them. The psychological term *displacement* means to displace anger from one object or person to another. It's easy to vent anger toward innocent people, or groups of people, instead of expressing our anger appropriately. Our mail carrier asked me one day (knowing I'm a pastor) where I thought racism comes from. I told her *racism* is just another word for *hatred*. It's wrong to lump groups of people together, stereotype them, and mistreat them. Racism comes from malice in the heart.

Malice says, "I hope they get what's coming to them." Malice wants to get even and to settle. Malice wishes misfortune on others. In that sense, malice is closely connected to envy and jealousy. Malice hopes for the worst, while love hopes for the best. It all comes from the sinful nature of humanity. The answer to malice is found in Galatians 5:24: "Those who [belong to Christ Jesus] have crucified the flesh with its passions and desires. If we live in the Spirit, let us also walk in the Spirit" (NKJV). We need to nail malice to the cross and receive a baptism of divine love in our hearts. Then the fruit of the Spirit, which is kindness, will grow in our lives.

Act Out

Finally, kindness is expressed most powerfully in the way we act toward others: "Be kind and compassionate to one another, forgiving each other, just as in Christ God forgave you" (Ephesians 4:32).

An allegory is told about Leonardo da Vinci's painting of *The Last Supper*. The story says Leonardo had a sharp disagreement with a fellow painter just before he began his work on the famous painting. Out of anger he decided to use the face of that man as the face of Judas Iscariot in his painting. He painted his resentment in the facial expression of Judas.

However, the artist lost his inspiration when he came to paint the face of Jesus. He struggled to capture what Jesus must have felt the night He faced the cross. His unforgiveness blocked his inspiration. So, Leonardo repented of his resentment and forgave the man in his heart. He repainted the face of Judas and removed the image of the man with whom he was angry. Then the flow of inspiration returned and he finished his masterpiece.

We cannot paint the features of Jesus into our life while painting others with the colors of anger and resentment. We must forgive and bear the fruit of kindness.

6
FOR GOODNESS' SAKE

Mother Teresa said, "Maybe you can't do great things for God. But you can do good things with a great heart." The Greek word for *goodness* describes someone or something that is excellent and beneficial. *Goodness*, then, means the highest quality and character. It also means to be kind and merciful—someone who is good in their nature and good in their actions toward others. Most importantly, God is good!

This Greek word for "goodness" (*agathos*) in the Bible is not found in classical Greek literature. In some respects, this is a unique Biblical word. It's a unique spiritual value. Goodness is vital for our mental health and productive relationships. While we talk about original sin, we also need to know about our original goodness. God created us in His image. Human nature has an inherent, God-created goodness. While we do have a sin nature, we are also made in God's likeness. God created us in His goodness and with His goodness. At the dawn of Creation, "God saw all that he has made, and it was very good" (Genesis 1:31). That includes you and me!

The fruit of the Spirit is goodness. Jesus said, "Every good tree bears good fruit" (Matthew 7:17). He also pointed out, "The good man brings good things out of the good stored up in him, and the evil man brings evil things out of the evil stored up in him" (12:35). Character is the sum total of what's stored up in us—our attitudes, values, beliefs, and behavior. When we're good on the inside, it comes out. A good heart produces good speech, good actions, and good relationships.

In the parable of the sower, Jesus described people with "a noble and good heart, who hear the word, retain it, and by persevering produce a crop" (Luke 8:15). A good heart is open and receptive to hearing and receiving the Word of God. A person with a good heart listens to God's Word and receives its counsel, correction, and comfort. But a person with a bad heart gets angry about truth, resists the Holy Spirit, and rejects the Word of God. The good heart is teachable and submissive. "But the wisdom that comes from heaven is first of all pure; then peace-loving, considerate, submissive, full of mercy and good fruit, impartial and sincere" (James 3:17). The good soil represents the condition of a heart that is receptive to God's Word.

Goodness also describes Christian morality. "Love must be sincere. Hate what is evil, cling to what is good" (Romans 12:9). Genuine love hates what is evil. It doesn't hate people, but it hates and rejects things that are harmful and bad. We must hold tightly to our faith in Christ and the timeless truths of the Bible, and reject the moral relativism of our day. We must cling to the good things that come to us from the Lord. "How much more will your Father who is in heaven give good things to those who ask Him!" (Matthew 7:11 NKJV).

Hate is a strong word. It means to utterly despise and reject something to the point that we have nothing to do with it. For example, I hate okra! I hate it in any shape, form, or fashion. I hate okra served in any amount, including a tad hidden in vegetable soup. Before I order vegetable soup at a restaurant, I ask, "Does it contain okra?" If it does, I refuse it even if the server tries to convince me how good the soup tastes. Some have gone so far as to say, "It doesn't even taste like okra."

Yes, it does! I hate okra baked, fried, or broiled. Why? First, because okra was not made for human consumption! Second, because my mother made me sit at the dinner table for over an hour one night until I ate the boiled okra she prepared for supper. I refused. My perseverance prevailed to the point that she finally gave up. I tried one small bite and immediately knew I hated it with a passion. In the same way, let's hate what is evil and cling to what it good.

Goodness makes us victorious when faced with evil, persecution, and injustice. "Do not be overcome by evil, but overcome evil with good" (Romans 12:21). When someone attacks you verbally, mistreats you, or gossips about you, don't stoop to their level and retaliate with the same kind of bad behavior. Rise above your hurt and choose the more excellent way by responding with goodness. When you do, the light of Jesus will shine through you! You can conquer evil with good.

Galatians 6:10 says, "Let us do good to all people, especially to those who belong to the family of believers."

We are members of the family of God and should treat everyone, especially our brothers and sisters in Christ, with goodness.

Goodness is the Christian standard for life: "Do not imitate what is evil but what is good" (3 John 11). Jesus is our mentor, so let's imitate Him. When we were kids, we imitated people. The art of imitation is the secret to learning. Education is the imitation of our teachers. The root meaning of *education* is to mimic. If we follow culture, we will imitate the world. So, we are told clearly, "Do not conform any longer to the pattern of this world" (Romans 12:2). If we follow Christ, we will imitate Him. Jesus said, "I have set you an example that you should do [to others] as I have done for you" (John 13:15).

Make sure the people you admire and look up to are good people. Make sure the media you watch and the news you follow are good in nature. If you allow bad people to influence your worldview, politics, spirituality, and morals, you will imitate what is bad. If you follow good people, you will imitate what is good. We get influenced in subtle, unconscious ways that we don't even realize. Let's follow good people who set good examples so we can imitate what is good.

The fruit of goodness is, most importantly, a word that describes the very nature of God. The Bible is filled with verses about the goodness of God, who declares, "I the Lord do not change" (Malachi 3:6). "Jesus Christ is the same yesterday and today and forever" (Hebrews 13:8). God is not good on some days and bad on other days. God is not good to you one day and mean toward you the next. God is not bipolar! The psalmist David praised God's goodness: "I am still confident of this: I will see the goodness of the Lord in the land of the living" (Psalm 27:13). Regardless of all his difficulties, David remained confident of the goodness of God because He never changes. Life is bad at times, but God is good. His presence, power, and peace are with us even when times are bad.

Don't give up your faith in tough times. Don't fall into negative thinking and a depressed outlook on your situation. Believe God for good things! The goodness of God is the reason I never give up. Regardless of how bad things get, God provides good gifts to His children. Psalm 23, which begins, "The Lord is my shepherd" (v. 1), is the most famous psalm. Encourage yourself by knowing this psalm and quoting it often. "Surely goodness and mercy shall follow me all the days of my life," David wrote (v. 6 NKJV). When you know God personally, you can say, "Oh, taste and see that the Lord is good" (34:8). When you receive Jesus Christ as your Savior and live by faith in His promises, you will taste for yourself and see the goodness of God in your life.

An Old Testament prophet declared, "The Lord is good, a stronghold in the day of trouble" (Nahum 1:7 NKJV). Nahum lived in troubled times. There was a lot of political trouble, national trouble, and economic trouble just like we face today. Yet, Nahum said, "The Lord is good." Life is difficult. Times are hard. Bad people do bad things. Yet, in every circumstance, the Lord is a stronghold in the day of trouble. A *stronghold* is a fortress to which we can run for shelter and safety when we are under attack. A stronghold is a safe place. Martin Luther wrote: "A mighty fortress is our God, A bulwark never failing."

Jesus emphasized the goodness of God:

"Ask and it will be given to you; seek and you will find; knock and the door will be opened to you. For everyone who asks receives; he who seeks finds; and to him who knocks, the door will be opened. Which of you, if his son asks for bread, will give him a stone? Or if he asks for a fish, will give him a snake? If you, then, though you are evil, know how to give good gifts to your children, how much more will your Father in heaven give good gifts to those who ask him!" (Matthew 7:7-11).

Every blessing we experience comes from the goodness of God. One of my favorite Bible verses is James 1:17: "Every good and perfect gift is from above, coming down from the Father of the heavenly lights, who does not change like shifting shadows." Take everything with gratitude from the hand of God, and never take anything for granted. Every good and perfect thing in your life comes from the hand of God.

When we produce the fruit of goodness, we make the world a better place to live. Goodness benefits everyone and everything. Goodness improves marriages, strengthens families, enhances work environments, and brings revival to the church.

Practical Guide

Barnabas—a key leader in the early church—was "a good man, full of the Holy Spirit and faith" (Acts 11:24a). Through his goodness, "a great number of people were brought to the Lord" (v. 24b).

After the Day of Pentecost, the church grew rapidly. The Gospel reached the city of Antioch in modern-day Turkey, where a great revival broke out and many people became Christians. News reached the apostles in Jerusalem, so they sent Barnabas to check out what was going on. "When he arrived and saw the evidence of the grace of God, he was glad and encouraged them all to remain true to the Lord with all their hearts" (v. 23).

Barnabas brought Saul with him to Antioch because he believed in him and saw his potential. He brought Saul to the forefront, where God began to use him in a powerful way. "So for a whole year Barnabas and Saul met with the church and taught great numbers of people. The disciples were called Christians first at Antioch" (vv. 26-27).

Barnabas was a Levitical priest whose real name was Joseph. He came from the island of Cyprus. After the Day of Pentecost, Barnabas heard the gospel of Christ and became a Christian. In fact, a lot of Jewish priests became Christians. "So the word of God spread. The number of disciples in Jerusalem increased rapidly, and a large number of priests became obedient to the faith" (Acts 6:7).

Barnabas sold some property he owned and made a significant contribution to the newborn church. The apostles gave him the nickname *Barnabas*, which means "son of encouragement," or "one summoned to help" (Greek, *parakletos*). It is the same word Jesus used to call the Holy Spirit the "Comforter" or "Counselor."

The apostles were impressed with his helpfulness and encouragement they saw in Barnabas, recognizing the Holy Spirit was at work in his life. Barnabas didn't need to be number one—he was a helper. He didn't seek promotions but sought to promote others. So, he promoted

THE BEST VERSION OF YOU

the Apostle Paul. He didn't need public applause. He was a mighty force for God as a man behind the scenes. He was a leader because he was a good man who helped others reach their potential in Christ.

Viewpoint

Barnabas had the right viewpoint of people. Goodness looks for evidence of the grace of God in others. Good people are never fault-finders but grace-finders! When he met the new Christians in Antioch, he "saw the evidence of the grace of God" (Acts 11:23). Great leaders look for the good in others. Barnabas saw the evidence of the new birth, the work of the Holy Spirit, and the power of the Gospel in Antioch. Good-natured people look for the evidence of grace. They look at people with eyes of grace, not eyes of judgment. Goodness sees the good in others before it sees anything else. When Barnabas saw grace at work, he was glad and encouraged others. We, too, need to see the best in others and encourage their strengths before we try to help them correct their weaknesses.

Our viewpoint determines how we treat the people in our life. Barnabas was looking for the evidence of God's grace in the hearts of the believers in Antioch. We see what we're looking for. Some people look for evidence to accuse us, criticize us, or discredit us. Religious leaders of Jesus' day looked for evidence to accuse Him of wrongdoing and false teaching. When they found none, they falsified evidence. They would ask Him questions in public only to try to trap Him by His answer (but they always failed!).

People today are quick to look at social media filled with gossip and accusation to find one thing they can quote or misquote against someone. You may have somebody very competitive with you at work who doesn't like you. They're always looking for some reason to accuse you or blame you. You may have somebody in your family who looks for reasons to criticize you. They're looking for the bad.

When we are born again, we have a new measure of spiritual love in our hearts that looks for the good in others. "The sinful mind is death, but the mind controlled by the Spirit is life and peace" (see Romans 8:6). The sinful mind looks for the bad in others, but the spiritual mind looks for the good. We need to train ourselves to look for the good just like Barnabas did. Let's find the good and encourage it in our family and friends. Overlook the bad, and look for the evidence of the grace of God.

True to the End

One way we show goodness is to encourage others. The word *encourage* means to "strengthen" someone. Specifically, Barnabas "encouraged them all to remain true to the Lord with all their hearts" (Acts 11:23). That's my encouragement to you: Remain true to the Lord with all your heart. Don't just include Jesus in your life; instead, give Him your life. Remaining true means to be faithful. True friends are faithful. Marriage is built on faithfulness to the covenant. Parents are faithful to raise their children in the training and instruction of the Lord. Strong churches are built on faithful members who give, serve, and pray.

The phrase "with all their hearts" describes a deep love, passion, and devotion. The Christian faith is the religion of the heart. It's more than practicing religious rituals, adhering to beliefs, and espousing a creed. "Love the Lord your God with all your heart" (Deuteronomy 6:5). God says, "You will seek me and find me when you seek me with all your heart" (Jeremiah 29:13). "Whatever you do, work at it with all your heart, as working for the Lord, not for [people]. . . . It is the Lord Christ you are serving" (Colossians 3:23-24). Your life will make a great impact if you remain true to the Lord with all your heart.

Technology is an amazing tool we have to preach the Gospel to the world. The prophet Habakkuk spoke of a time when "the earth will be filled with the knowledge of the glory of the Lord, as the waters cover the sea" (2:14). Jesus said, "This gospel of the kingdom will be preached in the whole world" (Matthew 24:14). Use the tool of social media to share Christ. Encourage the people in your life to believe in Jesus. When your Christian friends get discouraged, encourage them to remain true to the Lord with all their heart.

Bring Out the Best

Barnabas' greatest achievement was soliciting the partnership of Saul of Tarsus. The gift of encouragement Barnabas gave to Saul helped to transform him into the man we know as Paul the apostle. After Saul's dramatic conversion to Christ on the Damascus road, he returned to his home in Tarsus, not too far from the revival taking place in Antioch. Barbie and I have traveled to both cities in our Biblical study trips to Turkey. We have conducted worship services in these ancient cities and reflected on the birth of the early church.

Saul of Tarsus was an angry religious leader of his day. He rejected Jesus. In fact, he was there when Stephen, the first martyr of the church, was killed in the streets of Jerusalem. "And Saul was there, giving approval to his death. On that day a great persecution broke out against the church at Jerusalem, and all except the apostles were scattered. . . . But Saul began to destroy the church. Going from house to house, he dragged off men and women and put them in prison" (Acts 8:1-3). What heartbreaking words!

Yet, that dangerous, hate-filled man met Jesus face-to-face in a vision while on his way to Damascus to excommunicate Christians from the synagogue. Blinded by the dazzling light of glory, he could only see the face of Jesus and hear His convicting voice: "Saul, Saul, why do you persecute me?" (People don't persecute Christians—they actually persecute Jesus when they attack and criticize the church.) Terrified, Saul asked, "Who are you, Lord?" (9:4-5a).

Jesus replied, "I am Jesus, whom you are persecuting. . . . Now get up and go into the city, and you will be told what you must do" (vv. 5b-6). No one else in Saul's entourage saw the light or heard the voice of Jesus. Saul was taken to a house where he stayed for three days. A Christian leader named Ananias came to pray for him at the Lord's direction, and Saul's sight was restored. He was filled with the Holy Spirit and then baptized. He spent several days with the disciples in Damascus. Then listen to this amazing statement: "At once he began to preach in the synagogues that Jesus is the Son of God" (v. 20). Talk about a turnaround! The amazing grace of God transformed him immediately from persecution to preaching, from Judaism to Jesus, from law to grace, from imprisoning people to setting them free, from destroyer to disciple!

However, many people discredited his conversion as being a ruse to infiltrate the ranks of the church in a covert attempt to destroy it. Remember, this is the man who had been "breathing out murderous threats against the Lord's disciples" (9:1). The church feared Saul of Tarsus. He was public-enemy number one to the Gospel. They thought his conversion was false. They didn't trust him. "When he came to Jerusalem, he tried to join the disciples, but they were all afraid of him, not believing that he really was a disciple" (v. 26).

Can you imagine accepting Christ and then, when you try to join the church, they accuse you of not being a true Christian? Can you imagine the pastor of a church accusing you of desiring church membership because you have an evil intent to destroy the church? Well, that's what happened to Saul. How discouraging and deflating. Saul was reaping the anger and fear he had sown.

Now Barnabas entered the story. At this low point of Saul being mistrusted by the apostles, Barnabas defended him. "But Barnabas took him and brought him to the apostles" (v. 27a). He stepped in and he stepped up to defend the conversion of Saul as legitimate. That's the spiritual fruit of goodness in operation. He told the apostles how Saul had truly seen the Lord and how he "preached fearlessly in the name of Jesus" (v. 27b).

Saul stayed with the apostles for a while in Jerusalem and learned much about Jesus from their experiences.

Finally, the apostles accepted Saul because Barnabas validated him. However, when Saul returned home to Tarsus for a few years, he was not very active in ministry there, as far as we know. He probably preached to and taught anyone who would listen to him, but he did not get off to an easy start in his ministry. Many people were still doubtful of his conversion and fearful of his motives.

Barnabas saw the evidence of grace in Saul of Tarsus. He stirred up the gift of God he saw in him. Years later Paul encouraged Timothy, his son in the faith, to "stir up the gift of God which is in you" (2 Timothy 1:6 NKJV). We need people to stir up the gift of God in us, and we need to return the favor. Jesus redeemed Saul from sin, but the Lord used Barnabas to help turn him into Paul the apostle. That's why Barnabas is called "a good man" (Acts 11:24). Good people make others better. So, when Barnabas saw the opportunity in Antioch to build a church, he got Paul to help. That's when Paul emerged as an apostle in the early church and began carrying the Gospel to the Gentile nations.

Goodness not only sees the best in others; it brings out the best in them as well. Anyone can see the guilt, but it takes a good person to see the grace in us. The grace of God is often buried beneath the surface like it was in Saul. But Barnabas drew the gift of God out of Saul like drawing water from a well. "The purposes of a man's heart are deep waters, but a man of understanding draws them out" (Proverbs 20:5).

While the Holy Spirit works to produce the fruit of goodness, we must stop fault-finding and judging others. We need to resist the sinful nature that looks for the bad and instead ask the Holy Spirit to make us encouragers.

Who do you know that needs encouragement? If they've been knocked down, pick them up. If they've been criticized, speak up for them. If they've been overlooked, give them an opportunity. Don't let them stay home like Saul did in Tarsus. Go get them involved in life and ministry. You can be a Barnabas—an encourager—to someone today.

Stick With It

Leadership requires perseverance with people and never giving up on them. That's another quality about goodness we learn from Barnabas. "So for a whole year Barnabas and Saul met with the church and taught great numbers of people. The disciples were first called Christians at Antioch" (Acts 11:25-26).

Why is it significant that they stayed in Antioch? The apostles sent Barnabas to Antioch for a few days to check out the legitimacy of the newborn church, but Barnabas went way beyond the call of duty. He was also wise enough not to ask them for permission before he got Saul to help him. He knew they would probably be skeptical of his plan because of the suspicion many had about Saul. It's easier to ask for forgiveness than permission! Real leaders take initiative and have the courage to make decisions. Whatever your job description is at work, go beyond the call of duty. Whatever your ministry is at church, go beyond the call of duty. Whatever your role is at home, go beyond the call of duty.

In the Sermon on the Mount, Jesus said if someone compels you to go with them one mile, go the second mile. If someone asks for your coat, give them your overcoat as well. He said if somebody wants to borrow money from you, lend it without expecting to get it back (Matthew 5:40-42). As Christians we don't just do what's expected of us; we go beyond the call of duty. The Christian life is one of utmost excellence, diligent work, and courageous leadership. Such is the power of goodness at work in and through us as we are filled with the Holy Spirit.

7
FAITHFULLY YOURS

Cal Ripken Jr. is known as the "Iron Man of Baseball." He played 21 seasons with the Baltimore Orioles. He didn't have the greatest batting average, but he holds one statistic that distinguishes him from all other players. He never missed a professional baseball game for 21 years, playing 2,632 games consecutively. That enabled him to beat the former champion, Lou Gehrig, who previously held the record by playing 2,130 consecutive games. When major-league teams honored Ripken from stadium to stadium, fans stood to their feet and cheered loudly, commending him for his faithfulness.

Spiritual growth produces the spiritual fruit of faithfulness. Just like a farmer looks for fruit on his trees, Jesus looks for spiritual fruit on the trees of our lives. "This is to my Father's glory, that you bear much fruit, showing yourselves to be my disciples" (John 15:8). The word *faithfulness* simply means "full of faith." Jesus asked, "When the Son of Man comes, will he find faith on the earth?" (Luke 18:8). He's looking for the fruit of faith!

It's important that we connect what we believe with how we live. Faith is a way of living as well as a way of believing. "We live by faith, not by sight" (2 Corinthians 5:7). If we truly believe Jesus is Lord, we will be faithful to Him, His teachings, His church, and His calling. If we believe God exists and He is our heavenly Father, we will be faithful to Him. If we believe the Holy Spirit lives in our hearts to empower and counsel us, we will depend on Him. If we believe the Bible is the inspired Word of God, we will be faithful to read it and take it to heart. If we believe in the power of prayer, we will be faithful to pray.

Faithfulness means to be steady. We live in an unstable world. Yet, the Holy Spirit enables us to be steady in the storm! Everything that can be shaken is being shaken, but "we are receiving a kingdom that cannot be shaken" (Hebrews 12:28). The faithful person is reliable, dependable, and trustworthy. It also means to be truthful and honest. When we're faithful, people can count on us. When we're faithful, we keep our word.

God rewards faithfulness. "To the faithful," God shows Himself to be "faithful" (2 Samuel 22:26). Psalm 97:10 says, "[God] guards the lives of his faithful ones." God is our 24/7 security system! God "protects the way of his faithful ones" (Proverbs 2:8), and "the Lord will richly bless the faithful" (see 28:20).

Someday, each of Jesus' faithful followers can expect to hear Him say, "Well done, good and faithful servant! You have been faithful with a few things; I will put you in charge of many things. Come and share your master's happiness!" (Matthew 25:21). Those words are the ultimate measure of true success. We don't measure success by power, possessions, or position. Our ultimate success is when we stand before Jesus and hear Him say, "Well done, good and faithful servant!"

The Holy Spirit encourages and enables us to be faithful. We need to commit ourselves to faithfulness in our relationships and responsibilities. Faithfulness is an indispensable core value. Faithfulness is possible for everyone to achieve. Faithfulness can also be difficult and may come at a cost. We need to pray, *Holy Spirit, empower me and help me to be faithful, truthful, honest, reliable, dependable, steady, and full of faith.*

Loyal Love

The Christian experience is different from religion. While we may inherit religious practices from our upbringing, we must make a personal choice to follow Christ. Faith in Jesus means faithfulness to Him. Jesus is always faithful to us. Paul wrote, "If we are faithless, he [Jesus] will remain faithful" (2 Timothy 2:13). Our highest loyalty, as Christians, is to be faithful to Christ. I pray that you have received Christ as your Savior and are following Him as Lord.

The church at Smyrna faced persecution, but Jesus told them, "Be faithful, even to the point of death, and I will give you the crown of life" (Revelation 2:10). Christians throughout history and even today around the world are persecuted. Some have made the ultimate sacrifice by giving their lives for the cause of Christ. "They did not love their lives so much as to shrink from death" (Revelation 12:11).

Never disown Jesus. Never deny Him. Never depart from Him. He will be faithful to you to the very end. God is "able to keep you from falling and to present you before his glorious presence without fault and with great joy!" (Jude 24).

Marriage Covenant

Marriage is a sacred institution for God's purpose of continuing the human story. When the nation of Israel was restored after the Babylonian Captivity, God sent a great revival that resulted in social reforms. Marriage had lost its purpose during their exile. They had adopted the pagan ways of Babylon. Marriage was not taken seriously—commitments and vows were easily broken. The men were unfaithful to their wives. The prophet Malachi called them back to a Biblical view of marriage.

Marriage is the foundation of the family. When the foundation cracks, the whole house falls. Biblical marriage is specifically defined as a sacred relationship between one man and one woman. Today, we see a cultural distortion of this Biblical standard. While the world may change its views, a godly marriage will always be a sacred relationship between a man and woman in a covenant before God. We follow Christ, not culture; Scripture, not society. We follow God's Word regarding marriage, not the ways of this world. "The world and its desires pass away, but the man who does the will of God lives forever" (1 John 2:17).

The Bible gives this definition of *marriage*: "For this reason a man will leave his father and mother and be united to his wife, and they will become one flesh" (Genesis 2:24; also see Mark 10:7-8). This is the only Biblical definition for marriage; any other configuration is outside the will of God. Christians are clearly told, "Do not conform . . . to the pattern of this world" (Romans 12:2), and that includes worldly views of marriage. The foundation of a healthy marriage is faithfulness. It is more important than compatibility, romance, and communication, which are also very important. Faithfulness provides the foundation for a marriage that lasts.

The prophet Malachi confronted the breakdown of marriage: "The Lord is acting as the witness between you and the wife of your youth, because you have broken faith with her, though she is your partner, the wife of your marriage covenant" (Malachi 2:14). He called the men to make a new commitment of faithfulness: "So guard yourself in your spirit, and do not break faith with the wife of your youth" (v. 15).

Marriage is a covenant, not a contract. A *contract* is a legal agreement that can easily be broken, altered, or negated. A *covenant* is a loving agreement permanently based on faithfulness. Divorce is the result of adultery, abandonment, or abuse, all of which are acts of unfaithfulness. In verse 16, Malachi repeated for emphasis, "So guard yourself in your spirit, and do not break faith." *Breaking faith* means breaking the marriage vow. Great marriages are built on keeping our vows and loving each other faithfully.

Faithful Families

We all were born into our natural family; we didn't get to pick our family. It's been said friends are God's apology for the family He gave us! As Christians, we also have a spiritual family—the church of Christ. The church is called the "family of believers" (Galatians 6:10).

We all face family problems and challenges. Families deal with dysfunctional behavior, health issues, financial problems, spiritual differences, and relational conflicts. Yet, we are called to love our family and to be faithful. Husbands must love and respect their wives. Wives must love and support their husbands. Parents must teach and nurture their children. Kids must honor and obey their parents. Healthy families are built on faithfulness to one another.

We need to provide for the family. "If anyone does not provide for his relatives, and especially for his immediate family, he has denied the faith and is worse than an unbeliever" (1 Timothy 5:8). While some people can't work because of disabilities, the Bible teaches us to earn income so we can provide for our family. This is a measure of our faithfulness.

Some people want others to provide for their family while they neglect their own household. Paul addressed this issue: "If any woman who is a believer has widows in her family, she should help them and not let the church be burdened with them, so that the church can help those widows who are really in need" (1 Timothy 5:16). While some look to the government to provide, God expects us to earn our own living so we can provide for our family.

When we help people to the point they become dependent, we aren't helping them at all. We need to empower others to make it on their own, rather than being dependent on continued assistance. While we provide for our kids, we need to teach them the work ethic so they will become productive as adults. True provision empowers kids to be faithful to work. My parents provided for us as kids, but they also taught us to work with household duties and also how to get a job when we were old enough to work.

When you get frustrated or disappointed with your family, don't give up on them. Don't disown, discard, or deny your family. Devote yourself afresh to be faithful to your family and do all you can do to help them even in the worst of times. Love "endures all things" (1 Corinthians 13:7 NKJV). Faithfulness requires us to endure many things as a family. When we persevere through marriage and family problems, we will see the power of God to give us victory in every battle we face.

Your Word Is Your Bond

Words are powerful. "We all stumble in many ways. If anyone is never at fault in what he says, he is a perfect man, able to keep his whole body in check" (James 3:2). That means no one is perfect! We say the wrong thing sometimes, or we say the right thing at the wrong time! Words don't always come out right, and we have to clean up the mess when they don't. Taming the tongue is the toughest challenge of life.

Texting, emails, and social media enable us to use more words than at any time in history. Effective communication requires wisdom on our part. "When words are many, sin is not absent, but he who holds his tongue is wise" (Proverbs 10:19). Also, "As a dream comes when there are many cares, so the speech of a fool when there are many words" (Ecclesiastes 5:3). What we need occasionally is to go on a word diet and lower the amount of our words. Use less words when you talk, and that will make you wiser in your conversations.

When words are many, we get careless in our communication. Jesus said, "[People] will have to give account on the day of judgment for every careless word they have spoken" (Matthew 12:36). The word *careless* in the Greek language describes words that are empty, powerless, ineffective, meaningless, and idle. On the contrary, "The word of God is living and active" (Hebrews 4:12). Our words should be living and active so that they bring people good, not harm; lifting up, not putting down; thoughtful, not thoughtless; kind, not harsh; loving, not hateful; smart, not stupid; mature, not childish; faith-filled, not doubtful; creative, not destructive; godly, not godless; pure, not profane; useful, not useless; anointed, not angry; merciful, not mean; gracious, not judgmental; forgiving, not judging; blessed, not bitter. Such words enrich our relationships.

Carefully consider the long-term effects of the promises you make. Then you will make the right commitments and not over-obligate yourself. We often make promises we can't keep, with good intentions. Barbie has told me many times, "Don't tell the kids 'maybe' when they ask if they can get something or do something, because *maybe* means yes to a kid. Tell them yes or no, but not maybe." Then she quotes Jesus to me: "Simply let your 'Yes' be 'Yes,' and your 'No' [be] 'No'; anything beyond this comes from the evil one" (Matthew 5:37).

So, be faithful to keep your word, even when it hurts. Ecclesiastes teaches us: "When you make a vow to God, do not delay in fulfilling it. . . . It is better not to vow than to make a vow and not fulfill it. . . . Much dreaming and many words are meaningless" (5:4-7). We are called to speak faithful words, not foolish words. Wise words bring a harvest of righteousness and a blessing in our lives. Our word is our bond that should be as binding as a legal contract. In fact, legal contracts can be based simply on a verbal commitment. The use of words also includes written as well as spoken words.

Our vows to God are the most important of all the vows we make. When Jonah ran away from God and got swallowed by a whale, he prayed and called on God to save him (which is a smart thing to do when you get swallowed up by the problems of life). Listen to his prayer: "'But I, with a song of thanksgiving, will sacrifice to you. What I have vowed I will make good. Salvation comes from the Lord.' And the Lord commanded the fish, and it vomited Jonah onto dry land" (Jonah 2:9-10). When he kept his vow, God delivered him from his predicament, and he got back on track doing God's will for his life.

True Friends

Close friends are faithful to each other. Faithfulness is the mark of a true friend. Now, we all have acquaintances—people we know, people we may even hang out with—but a true friend is one of the greatest blessings in life. Proverbs 17:17 puts it this way: "A friend loves at all times." We also learn: "There is a friend who sticks closer than a brother" (18:24). The key word is *stick*! Friends stick together through thick and thin! There's no variation in a friendship. Friends don't really get mad at each other. They don't have a falling out. Friends share a constant love that doesn't rise and fall on feelings, circumstances, or mistakes. Friends don't ever stop being friends. Friends are trusting and trustworthy, at all times. "Faithful are the wounds of a friend" (27:6 NKJV).

The price of friendship is confidentiality, trust, and loyalty. Jesus gave the gift of friendship to His disciples. They called Him, "Teacher," "Messiah," or "Lord." When He ministered the Last Supper, He said: "Greater love has no one than this, that he lay down his life for his friends.

THE BEST VERSION OF YOU

You are my friends if you do what I command. I no longer call you servants, because a servant does not know his master's business. Instead, I have called you friends, for everything that I learned from my Father I have made known to you" (John 15:13-15). Their relationship had grown from students to friends. Their relationship shifted from simply doing tasks to knowing the secrets of the kingdom of God, and from merely following Christ to loving Him.

When Jesus first met Peter the fisherman, He called him by saying, "Follow Me." After the Resurrection, when Peter had denied Him, Jesus asked him one essential question: "Do you love Me?"

Peter replied, "Lord, You know that I love You!"

Peter writes to every Christian: "Though you have not seen him [Jesus], you love him; and even though you do not see him now, you believe in him and are filled with an inexpressible and glorious joy" (1 Peter 1:8). Our faith in Christ blossoms in a love that is faithful to Him regardless of the cost of discipleship.

Faithful Work

We should be faithful at work. If we're going to produce and prosper, we must be faithful at our work. Paul the apostle commended the church at Thessalonica for their "work produced by faith" (1 Thessalonians 1:3). They were faithful in their work for the Lord. When people go to work, they shouldn't use company time to do personal things. I see people standing around at jobs looking at their cell phone when they should be doing the job they are paid to do.

Some people need to be supervised because they don't have the core value of faithfulness. When people have the core value of being faithful, they don't have to be supervised. Faithful people do the best work, go beyond the call of duty, and take the initiative to do what needs to be done without instruction because they are faithful. God honors faithfulness. It's the key to promotion! If you own a business, lead an organization, or manage workers, they will emulate your work ethic and your faithfulness. Sometimes people in organizations, corporations, and churches lack faithfulness because they see the people at the top not being faithful. Workers rise to the level of their leaders. Children rise to the level of their parents. Students rise to the level of their teachers. So, let's be faithful! Others are following in our footsteps.

Faithfulness inspires productivity, commitment, and diligence. "Whatever you do, work at it with all of your heart, as working for the Lord, not for [people], since you know that you will receive an inheritance from the Lord as a reward. It is the Lord Christ you are serving" (Colossians 3:23-24). The principle of working with all your heart is the key to success. Work with all your heart—work for the Lord, not just people—and you will receive a reward from the Lord. He will promote you and prosper you when you turn your work into your witness.

Faithful Giving

Wealth and worship are inseparable. Jesus said, "Where your treasure is, there your heart will be also" (Matthew 6:21). Our treasure and our heart travel together. They are inseparably connected. If our heart is in the church, we give to the church. If our heart is in missions, we will support the missionaries. If our heart cares for the poor, we help them. The Word of God teaches us to be faithful in our tithes, which is the first tenth of our income, and our offerings. An offering is a freewill expression of gratitude for God's blessings.

Tithing is an act of obedient worship, while offerings are expressions of personal praise. Offerings are given according to what we have "decided in [our] heart to give, not reluctantly or under compulsion, for God loves a cheerful giver" (2 Corinthians 9:7). We are also instructed to give to those in need. "Remember the poor" (Galatians 2:10). Jesus said, "When you give to the needy, do not let your left hand know what your right hand is doing, so that your giving may be in secret" (Matthew 6:3-4).

We don't give our tithes and offerings when we feel like it or sporadically, but consistently as we earn income. We give the first portion, not the last. We give our firstfruits, not our leftovers. "Honor the Lord with your wealth, with the firstfruits of all your crops" (Proverbs 3:9). We are to give our tithes and offerings as a part of our worship on the Lord's Day (1 Corinthians 16:2).

God promises to bless us abundantly when we give. "'Bring the whole tithe into the storehouse, that there may be food in my house. Test me in this,' says the Lord Almighty, 'and see if I will not throw open the floodgates of heaven and pour out so much blessing that you will not have room enough for it. I will prevent pests from devouring your crops, and the vines in your fields will not cast their fruit. . . . Then all the nations will call you blessed, for yours will be a delightful land,' says the Lord Almighty" (Malachi 3:10-12).

Three times in this passage God uses His name *El Shaddai*, "the Lord Almighty," to make a promise to bless our giving. This is the only place in the Bible where God invites us to test Him and see the powerful results of tithing and giving. God promises to prosper us and to prevent anything from devouring our lives or preventing us from being productive. If you test Him by tithing, you will step into a new realm of His blessings on your life.

The motive and purpose of tithing and giving is not to get something in return, even though God promises a return. We don't give to get. We give to give. Generosity is a virtue, and the real reward is the personal satisfaction that we are investing in the gospel of Christ. We are living the extended life. Giving gets us outside of ourselves. Giving is investing in something bigger than us. Giving delivers us from self-sufficiency because we trust God to give back what we gave up. Giving saves us from selfishness because we don't keep everything we earn for ourselves. Giving frees us from the fear of poverty and keeps us trusting God for our daily bread.

We give financially to build the church, to preach the Gospel, to care for the needy, to send missionaries, and to provide Christian hope and healing to the community and the world. Our giving enables the church to be the salt of the earth, the light of the world, and the city set on a hill providing a place of refuge for the world. Jesus promises a blessing for generosity: "Give, and it will be given to you. A good measure, pressed down, shaken together and running over, will be poured into your lap. For with the measure you use, it will be measured to you" (Luke 6:38). So, we get more than we give, but that's not the reason we give. We give to worship the Lord in gratitude for His blessings and to fulfill the Lord's commission for us to go into all the world and preach the good news of salvation in Christ.

I'm grateful for my parents who taught me faithful tithing and generous giving. My mother managed the money in our house, and taught me about spending wisely, saving consistently, and, most importantly, tithing faithfully. I can tell you by personal experience that God blesses tithing. If you tithe and support the church and the work of the ministry, you will look back over your life one day and see the investment you made in the kingdom of God. Your giving will be a testimony of your devotion to Christ and your concern for the spiritual welfare of others. Your giving makes the difference in the world.

Generosity enables you to live the extended life as you make a positive impact in the world for Christ. When you give, the church thrives, missionaries are sent, the poor are helped, disciples are made, care and counseling are provided, and the light of Christ shines brightly through His glorious church. Financial stewardship enables you to take something temporary (money) and turn it into something eternal—the salvation of humanity. "God is not unjust; he will not forget your work and the love you have shown him as you have helped his people and continue to help them" (Hebrews 6:10). God is faithful to bless the generosity of His people.

Church Life

Augustine, the early Christian leader and author of *Confessions* and *City of God*, said, "If God is our Father, the church is our mother." You can't have Christ without

His church. Christ is the head; the church is His body. The moment you accept Jesus, you're a member of His church. The church is "the family of believers" (Galatians 6:10). What a privilege it is to be a part of Christ's church! First Corinthians 12:27 says, "Now you are the body of Christ, and each one of you is a part of it." If we're faithful to Jesus, we'll be faithful to His church. Every local congregation is built by people who make a commitment to that body of believers of their time, talent, and treasure.

A strong church requires the faithfulness of the members. "Let us hold unswervingly to the hope we profess, for he who promised is faithful. And let us consider how we may spur one another on toward love and good deeds. Let us not give up meeting together, as some are in the habit of doing, but let us encourage one another—and all the more as you see the Day approaching" (Hebrews 10:23-25).

After the Day of Pentecost, when the church was born, they demonstrated faithfulness. They didn't just live on the emotional high of the Holy Spirit's fresh anointing. Emotion turned into endurance! "They devoted themselves to the apostles' teaching and to the fellowship, to the breaking of bread and to prayer" (Acts 2:42). Churches thrive when the people are faithful. "Day after day, in the temple courts and from house to house, they never stopped teaching and proclaiming the good news that Jesus is the Christ" (5:42). Christians are called to gather for worship and fellowship and then to go into the community to shine the light of Christ. Jesus promised, "For where two or three come together in my name, there am I with them" (Matthew 18:20). We go to church to experience the special visitation of Jesus in our worship together.

Every member of the church is given spiritual gifts to serve the body of Christ. "From him [Jesus Christ] the whole body [of Christ], joined and held together by every supporting ligament [that's you and me], grows and builds itself up in love, as each part does its work" (Ephesians 4:16). You need to be faithful in your service so the body of Christ remains healthy and growing. "Each one should use whatever gift he [or she] has received to serve others, faithfully administering God's grace in its various forms" (1 Peter 4:10). All God's children are gifted children! Use your gifts to serve Christ and the church, and your life will make an eternal impact on the world.

Faithful in Prayer

The Word of God calls us to be faithful in prayer: "Devote yourselves to prayer, being watchful and thankful. And pray for us, too" (Colossians 4:2-3). God's people need to be "joyful in hope, patient in affliction, faithful in prayer" (Romans 12:12). When we pray, the world within us and around us changes for the better. So, "pray in the Spirit on all occasions with all kinds of prayers and requests. With this in mind, be alert [and self-controlled] and always keep on praying for all the saints" (Ephesians 6:18). We need more prayer in our hearts, in our homes, in our churches, in our schools, in our businesses, and in our nation. Prayer is so powerful that Jesus even taught us to "pray for those who mistreat you" (Luke 6:28). Don't ever quit praying as you remember Jesus' admonition that we "should always pray and not give up" (Luke 18:1).

Corrie ten Boom, survivor of the Holocaust, said, "Faithfulness is God's standard of success." We are facing uncertain times and unprecedented changes in our world. Yet, God is sovereign over history, and He is with us. Above all, we have been "predestined according to the plan of him who works out everything in conformity with the purpose of his will" (Ephesians 1:11). Jesus calls us to a life of faithfulness in faithless times.

While the world lives in fear, we live by faith. God put us here at this time in this generation, "in which [we] shine like stars in the universe as [we] hold out the word of life" (Philippians 2:15-16). This day "calls for patient endurance and faithfulness on the part of the saints" (Revelation 13:10). God will see us through and prosper us. God will use us mightily in this generation as we remain faithful. Jesus promises us: "Be faithful . . . and I will give you the crown of life" (Revelation 2:10).

As I'm writing this chapter, I'm sitting in a quiet corner of a coffee shop. A man I've never met just walked over to me and asked, "Pastor, what's a good word for today?"

I replied, "Here's a word for today: Jesus said to us His people, 'Be faithful . . . and I will give you the crown of life!' We can't always be perfect or be the best, but we can all be faithful to God, to each other, to our work, and our calling in life."

He said, "Thank you! That's exactly what I needed to hear today."

After our son David Paul was born, a friend gave me this poem to encourage me as a new father:

A careful man I want to be, a little boy follows me;

I do not care to go astray, for fear he may go the self-same way.

I cannot once escape his eye, whatever he sees me do he'll try;

*Like me he says he's going to be, this little boy who
    follows me.*

*He thinks that I am big and fine, believes in every
    word of mine;*

*That base in me he must not see, this little lad who
    follows me.*

*I must remember as I go, through summer suns and
    winter snow,*

*I'm building for the years to be, this little boy who
    follows me.*

Be faithful—someone is following you.

8
GENTLE TOUCH

Babe Ruth remains one of the most famous baseball players in history. He held the career record for the most home runs (714) for 39 years, until it was broken by Hank Aaron in 1974.

Near the end of his baseball career, Ruth was playing a poor game. He made several misplays that allowed the other team to score five runs in one inning, and he struck out. The manager had to take him out of the game.

The crowd booed Ruth as he left the field and headed toward the dugout. Suddenly, the story is told, a little boy ran onto the field and grabbed Ruth's leg. The slugger hugged the boy and walked off the field with him. That little boy gave Ruth the gift of gentleness at a low point. When we are down and out, having a bad performance at life, we too need someone to give us the gift of gentleness.

The fruit of the Holy Spirit is gentleness (Galatians 5:23). The Greek word for *gentleness* means to be "meek" or "humble," and is often translated this way in the New Testament. Aristotle, the noted philosopher, said gentleness is the balancing point between extreme anger and extreme passivity. Gentleness is emotional balance.

Feelings don't go over the edge in either direction. When we are gentle, we are able to keep control of our emotions, impulses, desires, and passions.

Gentleness is a divine attribute. Through the power of the indwelling Holy Spirit, we can overcome our frustration with others and give them the gift of gentleness. When we see someone fail, we should give them the gift of gentleness to encourage them and pick them up.

Power Under Control

Gentleness means to possess great power under great control. While we possess the power to act, we restrain that power. Moses had the God-given power of persuasion over Pharaoh and the people of Israel. Such divine power enabled him to lead the Israelites out of captivity, through the desert, and to the Promised Land. Moses is the most powerful prophet who ever lived. Yet, he was a humble person. He knew power belonged to God and came from God. Moses understood he operated on delegated power and must use that power only for God's purpose, never his own.

Numbers 12:3 says, "Moses was a very humble man, more humble than anyone else on the face of the earth." *Gentleness* means "meekness." Moses was the meekest man yet the most powerful prophet. Meekness is not weakness! Moses was a very passionate man, yet he was gentle. A gentle person is not someone with a flat-line personality. Gentleness doesn't mean a "go along to get along" attitude but, rather, great power under great control—mental, emotional, and physical control. Leadership doesn't mean to be domineering or overly demanding. The most effective leaders are visionary, driven, and passionate; but they are also gentle with the people they lead. They can challenge others without crushing their confidence. They can correct the mistakes of others in a way that develops them rather than destroying them.

When He lived on earth, Jesus was the ultimate example of gentleness. He had all power in Heaven and on earth, yet He said, "I am gentle and humble in heart" (Matthew 11:29).

When Jesus was interrogated by Pontius Pilate and King Herod, He remained silent. Pilate got frustrated with Jesus' silence and threatened Him.

"Where do you come from?" he asked Jesus, but Jesus gave him no answer. "Do you refuse to speak to me?" Pilate said. "Don't you realize I have power either to free you or to crucify you?" Jesus answered, "You would have no power over me if it were not given to you from above" (John 19:9-11).

Jesus possessed great power under great control!

Jesus had told His disciples of His power when He was arrested in the Garden of Gethsemane: "Do you think I cannot call on my Father, and he will at once put at my disposal more than twelve legions of angels? But how then would the Scriptures be fulfilled that say it must happen in this way?" (Matthew 26:53-54).

A Roman legion of soldiers was 6,000 men. So, Jesus could have called 72,000 warring angels. One angel of the Lord killed 185,000 Syrian soldiers one night in their campsite as they prepared to attack the city of Jerusalem (2 Kings 19:35). King Sennacherib and his troops retreated in defeat the next morning. He was assassinated by two of his own sons as soon as he arrived home. If one angel has the power to do that, think of what 72,000 could do! Yet, Jesus didn't summon the angels to rescue Him. He went willingly to the cross as the Lamb of God to take away the sins of the world. Great power under great control—what a Savior!

Submit to God's Will

The fruit of gentleness grows in our hearts when we submit to God's will. Gentle people are submissive to God rather than being stubborn. They treasure the will of God over self-will. They put others ahead of their own interests. Jesus said, "Whoever wants to become great among you must be your servant, and whoever wants to be first must be slave of all. For even the Son of Man did not come to be served, but to serve, and to give his life as a ransom for many" (Mark 10:43-45). If you are willing to be last, God will put you first. If you serve, you can then lead. Moses and Jesus were great leaders because they were gentle, humble, and submissive to God's will.

King Saul started great but finished poorly because he was stubborn. The power went to his head. He started off humble but fell into pride because he was a king. He should have honored the Lord God as the only King of Israel and served God's will. Instead, he blatantly turned away from God and disobeyed Him. The prophet Samuel told Saul that God had rejected him as king and would raise up a new king—a man after God's heart. In the face of Saul's rebellion, Samuel told him, "To obey is better than sacrifice, and to heed is better than the fat of rams. For rebellion is like the sin of divination, and arrogance like the evil of idolatry" (1 Samuel 15:22-23).

Spiritually, *gentleness* means submission to God's will. We get into a lot of trouble when we resist God's will.

"The Holy Spirit says: 'Today, if you hear [God's] voice, do not harden your hearts as you did in the rebellion, during the time of testing in the desert'" (Hebrews 3:7-8). Here we find an analogy to the doubt and disobedience of Israel when they failed to enter the Promised Land but, instead, wandered in the desert for 40 years. Their doubt led to disobedience.

What do we learn from their stubbornness? Two great truths—rebellion leads to ruin, and submission leads to success. "How much more should we submit to the Father of our spirits and live!" (Hebrews 12:9). Doing God's will is the secret to His blessings. "The world and its desires pass away, but the [person] who does the will of God lives forever" (1 John 2:17). Instead of resisting God's will, let's rejoice in His will and pray, "I desire to do your will, O my God" (Psalm 40:8).

We need to go with Jesus to the Garden of Gethsemane, get on our knees beside Him (instead of falling asleep like the disciples did), and pray the life-changing prayer, "Father . . . not my will, but yours be done" (Luke 22:42). When we live every day saying, "Lord, not my will but Yours be done," we will live a blessed life. If the disciples had been submitted instead of sleeping, they would have remained faithful to Jesus in His hour of need instead of running away in fear when Jesus got arrested. Doing God's will leads us to our divine destiny.

Jesus said, "Blessed are the meek, for they will inherit the earth" (Matthew 5:5). Meekness doesn't demand its own way, push its own agenda, or manipulate others for selfish gain or political aspiration. The pathway to promotion is gentleness. Blessed are the meek—they inherit the earth. They inherit the blessings of God. They inherit true success and significance in life.

Jesus said, "Come to me, all you who are weary and burdened, and I will give you rest. Take my yoke upon you and learn from me, for I am gentle and humble in heart, and you will find rest for your souls. For my yoke is easy and my burden is light" (Matthew 11:28-30).

Jesus calls us to take His yoke of gentleness and humility upon us. The yoke is a wooden device placed over the necks of a pair of oxen, so they walk and work together. One is the lead ox whom the submissive and younger ox follows and obeys. Jesus calls us to allow Him to put the yoke of His lordship on our necks so we can follow His lead. The neck is a symbol of the human will in submission to Christ. When we resist and rebel, we are stiff-necked rather than submissive. Stephen confronted the self-righteous leaders of his day: "You stiff-necked people, with uncircumcised hearts and ears! . . . You always resist the Holy Spirit!" (Acts 7:51).

We need a submissive neck that allows Jesus to put His yoke on us. We need to come under the guidance and protection of His lordship. Great news—Jesus' yoke is easy! The yokes of religion, self-righteousness, and sin are heavy; Jesus' yoke is light. When we take His yoke upon us and follow His lead, He will guide us into God's perfect plan for our life.

Restraint, Not Revenge

The character quality of gentleness means to show restraint instead of taking revenge. Our world is afflicted by people who are bent on revenge. They can't overlook anything. They can't forgive anything. They can't let any perceived insult or injustice go. They cling to their un-righteous rage like it's a security blanket. If they weren't angry, they would have no reason to get out of bed in the morning. They wake up mad and turn on the angry news and talk shows that only feed their revenge and suspicions of the motives of others. They develop a paranoia falsely believing that people don't like them or discriminate against them or treat them unjustly. They are constantly on the lookout for any offense, so they vent their self-justified rage. Then they get on their cell phone and tell a friend how they told somebody off and put them in their place. Like King Saul of old, they too have "played the fool" (1 Samuel 26:21 NKJV).

We are living in what is being called the *age of rage*. Angry people live to promote their anger. There's no grace or mercy in them. They're driven by self-centeredness. We see it in politics. Politicians are tearing up politics. Organized groups stir the pot of social unrest. If a protest isn't peaceful and doesn't result in progress, then it's a waste of time and only makes matters worse and deepens the divide. Rage and revenge deteriorate relationships, families, and society.

Godly gentleness is the only power that can restrain violence and keep us from lashing out. During the days of the Flood, "Noah found favor [grace] in the eyes of the Lord. Noah was a righteous man, blameless among the people of his time, and he walked with God. . . . Now the earth was corrupt in God's sight and was full of violence" (Genesis 6:8-11). The only answer to violence is the grace of God in our hearts that comes from walking with God. It's better to walk with God than to war in the streets. Real change starts in the human heart by getting right with God. Then we have the power to love our neighbor. Grace makes us righteous which, in turn, makes us peaceful. "The work of righteousness will be peace" (Isaiah 32:17 NKJV).

The character of Christ in us is gentleness. We possess great power under great control. We find joy in forgiving, not in fighting. When we are in Christ and He is in us, we restrain our anger and turn it into a positive force for constructive change. The power of the Holy Spirit gives us the ability to restrain our passions even when we get hurt or angry. Gentleness means showing restraint instead of taking revenge. When you get angry, act like you're anointed! Live up to your best self, not your worst self.

Act; don't react. Jesus said, "If someone strikes you on the right cheek, turn to him [or her] the other also" (Matthew 5:39). That doesn't mean to let people abuse you. Jesus is saying not to allow the actions of others to make you overreact. You can choose to act like Jesus no matter how someone treats you. Take the high road. When you do, you win. Overcome meanness with meekness. The Word of God teaches us: "A gentle answer turns away wrath" (Proverbs 15:1).

When you respond in kindness and gentleness, you can overlook the offense. If you refuse to get into conflict, the heat dies down and the anger subsides. "Without wood a fire goes out; without gossip a quarrel dies down" (Proverbs 26:20). Don't *get back* at people; rather, *give back* the God-given gift of gentleness. The meek are mighty. Those who remain calm in conflict and master their emotions are true leaders. "Do not be overcome by evil, but overcome evil with good" (Romans 12:21).

When evil comes your way, don't try to match it by saying or doing something wrong that you will later regret. Overcome evil with good. Act out of the goodness of Christ's character in you.

Information to Formation

Gentleness means to be teachable and open to learning instead of being set in our ways, close-minded, and resistant to new information. This is the information age. We learn so much so fast. Information is now more available to us than at any time in history. Learning is vital for living. So, we must not ever complete our education. We must keep learning! Information leads to formation. We live what we learn. Information inspires, illuminates, and influences us. We read and study the Bible so its information leads to our formation in Christ's image. We learn from our parents, friends, and mentors who shape our lives. We grow spiritually through significant relationships with influential people.

Effective teaching requires us to be teachable students. A good student is receptive to learning, while a poor student is resistant, uninterested, and biased with prejudices. Universities, media platforms, and TV talk shows do everyone an injustice when they shut down dialogue. Education is based on dialogue. To the contrary, indoctrination is based on dogma. King David prayed, "Open my eyes that I may see wonderful things in your law" (Psalm 119:18). David was teachable and eager to learn. Students learn from teachers, and the best teachers learn from their students. Parents learn from their kids. Pastors learn from their members. Employers learn from their employees, and vice versa.

Regardless of your position or prominence, you need to be eager to learn. "Make every effort to add to your faith" (2 Peter 1:5). If you don't add to your learning, a natural subtraction process takes place, and you forget what you've learned. If you don't believe that, try to help your kid with their algebra homework and you'll realize how much you've forgotten since high school! So, add to your learning with a gentle and teachable attitude and you will continue to grow in grace and knowledge.

Smart people keep learning. "Let the wise listen and add to their learning" (Proverbs 1:5). When you attend a course, a seminar, or listen to a sermon, don't tell yourself you already know the material. Rather, listen to learn something new about what you already know! You can always know something at a deeper level and apply it in a new way. Jesus often ended His teachings by saying, "Whoever has ears, let him hear." Progress in life is not based on what you already know but in learning what you don't know. That's how you grow. The word *gentleness* means the desire to learn new things and to gain new insights into old things.

We read in Proverbs 12:15, "The way of a fool seems right to him, but a wise man listens to advice." The term *fool* is used fourteen times in the Book of Proverbs. The fool is a caricature of a person who is devoid of spiritual insight, morals, and common sense. The fool thinks he knows everything, so he doesn't listen to anyone. The fool does what is right in his own eyes. The foolish mind is closed, while the mind of wisdom is open. A foolish person shows no interest in the things of God. "The message of the cross is foolishness to [them]" (1 Corinthians

1:18). We need to listen to the inner voice of the Holy Spirit, who guides us into all truth.

The fool is a person who has been fooled by misguided teachers and by the world system. If we challenge a foolish person, he or she will attack us. When we love each other, we are willing to listen to each other's viewpoint. Listening brings better understanding in our relationships. Listening is love in action and it shows respect to others.

When foolish people espouse foolish ideas, it makes the truth self-evident! Foolish people lack reason, logic, and objectivity. They confuse hysteria with history, feelings with facts, and superstition with science. The more they talk, the more you realize they don't know what they're talking about. If you ask them a reflective question, they get angry because they don't have a logical answer. The political world is full of foolish people in seats of government. That explains why their policies don't work or even make things worse.

The self-righteous mob that killed Stephen, the first Christian martyr, put their fingers in their ears and screamed at the top of their lungs so they didn't have to listen to his personal testimony (Acts 7:57). He recited the Old Testament prophecies of the Messiah, which they claimed to believe, but they were angry at the truth. He told them of his personal experience of salvation by faith in Jesus, but they refused to listen. As he defined his faith in Christ, they were convicted of their sins. Their misguided belief system was challenged by the authority of Scripture. They valued tradition over truth. The Gospel challenged "their truth." Instead of repenting, they raged at him. They dragged him into the street, and a mob ended his life, all because they refused to listen to the Gospel.

The age of rage in which we live is marked by shouting, looting, and violence in the name of social justice. Real justice makes life better, not worse. Liberty and justice exist for everyone, not just for the people with whom we agree. Silence is not complicity, as some people suggest. Silence is wisdom. When Jesus was insulted and falsely accused, He didn't say a word. In America we have the right to remain silent even in a court of law; how much more when we are engaged in conversation!

Angry people protest instead of working toward progress. Protesting is easy; progress is hard. They prefer conflict over conversation. They choose indoctrination over information. As Proverbs says, "Fools despise wisdom and discipline" (1:7), but "instruct a wise man and he will be wiser still" (9:9). The Apostle Paul spoke of the last days, when people will be "ever learning, and never able to come to the knowledge of the truth" (2 Timothy 3:7 KJV). A gentle person is teachable. Unteachable people, however, are anything but gentle.

A gentle person doesn't lash out at other people's opinions, views, and convictions. A gentle person listens and shows respect, even when they disagree. Listening shows respect for a person's right to their beliefs and viewpoints. The gospel of Christ is an announcement, not an argument. Once you establish a relationship with someone by respectful listening, you earn the right to share your faith with them. You reap what you sow. If you listen to them, they, in turn, will listen to you.

First Place

The gentle person puts others first. Gentleness is the character quality of putting others first. As we climb the ladder of success, let's take others with us to the top. Let's open the door for others instead of walking in first. Let's listen to their viewpoint instead of shutting them down. Let's allow the car on the road to cut in on our lane without getting mad about it. As the Scripture teaches: "Do nothing out of selfish ambition or vain conceit, but in humility consider others better than yourselves" (Philippians 2:3).

Leonard Bernstein, the great American composer and conductor, said "the second fiddle" is the most difficult musical instrument to play. "I can get plenty of first violins, but to find someone who can play the second fiddle with enthusiasm—that's a problem. And if we have no second fiddle, we have no harmony."

The Apostle Paul was given a great assignment by Jesus with great authority. When he wrote to the Corinthians with a strong appeal, he was motivated by love: "By the meekness and gentleness of Christ, I appeal to you. . . . For even if I boast somewhat freely about the authority the Lord gave us for building you up rather than pulling you down, I will not be ashamed of it" (2 Corinthians 10:1, 8). Paul could have made his appeal on the basis of his apostolic authority, but he suppressed the urge to power and chose rather to appeal to them out of love. Winning by intimidation is unspiritual and contrary to the character of Christ in us. We will get the best results in our relationships when we appeal to others with the meekness and gentleness of Christ. Affection is more powerful than authority. Authority without love is oppressive.

Early in my ministry, I was impressed while reading Paul's directive to ministers:

Don't have anything to do with foolish and stupid arguments, because you know they produce quarrels. And the Lord's servant must not quarrel; instead, he must be kind to everyone, able to teach, not resentful. Those who oppose him, he must gently instruct, in the hope that God will grant them repentance leading them to a knowledge of the truth, and that they will come to their senses and escape from the trap of the devil, who has taken them captive to do his will (2 Timothy 2:23-26).

Gentleness frees us from arguing, quarreling, or growing resentful because people don't agree with us. Gentle ministers know that when the seed of the Word of God is planted in a person's heart and mind, it will produce a result.

The gospel of Christ is the most powerful force in the world. The Gospel is a divine announcement, not a human argument. We don't need to defend the Gospel because it defends itself. We need to declare it! The Word does the work! "For the word of God is living and active" (Hebrews 4:12). So, whether you're a minister preaching in a church, a parent reading a Bible story to your kids, or a supervisor giving a devotion to your coworkers, "preach the Word; be prepared in season and out of season" (2 Timothy 4:2). When you trust the power of God's Word, you won't have to worry so much or work so hard to influence the people you love. The Word works! Show respect to the religious and unreligious, to the faithful and the faithless, to the churched and the unchurched. Effective ministry is conducted in the meekness and gentleness of Christ.

A class of elementary students were studying the Quakers as a part of American history. They learned they are meek and mild people who avoid conflict and always stay calm. The teacher asked each student to write a summary paragraph about the Quakers. One boy wrote: "Quakers are very meek and mild people who never argue, fight, or get angry. My father is a Quaker, but my mother is something else!"

All of us act out of our emotions. We vent our anxiety and our anger. So, when someone insults you, overlook it. When someone fails spiritually, restore them gently. When you get the opportunity to share your faith, be respectful of others' beliefs or lack thereof. Keep great power under great control. Be confident in your knowledge but also be teachable. Turn the other cheek. Put others first. Lay down your life. Lead others by serving them. When passions are running high, whisper this prayer:

Lord Jesus, take away my anxiety and my anger. Give me a special anointing to show Your meekness and gentleness to others. My highest purpose in life is to serve others in love so they may see Christ in me, the hope of glory.

9
TAKE CONTROL

Mark Twain, American author and humorist, said, "I've had more trouble with myself than any person I've ever met." He was talking about self-control. Psychologists tell us *self-control* is the ability to discipline and control our impulses, our emotions, and our behaviors in order to reach our goals.

When the Bible uses the term *self-control*, it means "self-mastery" and "temperance." In ancient Greek literature, *temperance* was used to describe a king or a ruler who put the interests of the people over his own interests. Self-control is the ability to put others first and, in that sense, means to curb self-indulgence.

When Paul was arrested and called to testify before Felix the governor, the apostle spoke to him about "righteousness, self-control and the judgment to come" (Acts 24:25a). As he listened, Felix trembled with conviction as he considered such great virtues. But he made the mistake of telling Paul, "Enough for now! I will call for you at a more convenient time" (see v. 25b).

The Greek word for *temperance* is used in 1 Corinthians 9:25 to describe athletes: "Everyone who competes in the games goes into strict training." Athletes are disciplined to win a reward that lasts a short time, but we do it to get a reward that will last forever. Self-control is needed to win at the game of life.

Self-control protects us from panic attacks. "God did not give us a spirit of timidity, but a spirit of power, of love and of self-discipline" (2 Timothy 1:7). The King James Version translates *self-discipline* as "a sound mind." A sound mind is one of disciplined thoughts. Don't let your thoughts run wild. Take them captive to the promises of God's Word.

The Apostle Peter instructed believers, "Be clear minded and self-controlled so that you can pray" (1 Peter 4:7). He added, "Be self-controlled and alert. Your enemy the devil prowls around like a roaring lion looking for someone to devour. Resist him, standing firm in the faith" (5:8-9). *Self-control* is the ability to govern our desires, decisions, and disciplines. The Holy Spirit doesn't control us in the sense of manipulating us. He gives us grace to control ourselves so we can live victoriously.

Set Goals

Self-control comes from setting goals. We need to set both short-term and long-range goals. Short-sightedness leads to immediate gratification. Immediate gratification of our impulses and desires gets us into trouble. Indulgence keeps us from achieving our goals. The world system tempts us to indulge our appetite and desires—to live it up! The world markets products and services that appeal to our desires. "For everything in the world—the cravings of sinful man, the lust of his eyes, and the boasting of what he has and does—comes not from the

Father but from the world. The world and its desires pass away, but the man who does the will of God lives forever" (1 John 2:16-17).

If you are driving your car and turn loose of the steering wheel, you'll crash. The car won't keep itself on course by itself. Self-control is the steering wheel of your life. While sin has its "pleasures," they last "a short time" (Hebrews 11:25). You may get immediate gratification, but you'll suffer negative long-term results.

By setting goals, we can develop self-control in order to reach them. Discipline reigns over desires and keeps us on track to fulfill our highest purpose. We need to discipline our time, talents, and our temperament. Goal-setting without goal-reaching is pointless. Self-control of our time, energy, and resources empowers us to turn dreams into reality and goals into accomplishments.

Write It Down

Realistic and reachable goals are clear and specific. Write down your goals and list them in order of importance. Until you write down a goal, it's only an idea. Written goals that you review every day will keep you moving forward. When God gave the Old Testament prophet Habakkuk a vision of history to come, He said, "Write down the revelation [vision] and make it plain on tablets so that a herald [messenger] may run with it. For the revelation awaits an appointed time; it speaks of the end and will not prove false. Though it linger, wait for it; it will certainly come and will not delay" (Habakkuk 2:2-3).

So, God was using "tablets" long before the Apple computer came along! God put His Word in writing! That's why we have the Bible.

Until a vision is written down, it is not plain. Unwritten goals are vague and ambiguous. Real goals are clear and concise—so write down goals and review them every day. Also, set a time frame to reach the goals. Ambiguity creates anxiety, while clarity brings confidence and peace. Written goals also enable you to wait for the vision to come to pass.

God told Habakkuk to write down the vision so a messenger could run with it. God can use you in your family, work, and ministry to launch a vision with strategic goals so others may run with it!

Self-Starters

Strategic goals are born in the hearts of self-starters. Goals start with you, and you've got to keep yourself fired up. "Fan into flame the gift of God, which is in you" (2 Timothy 1:6). When you go camping and the fire goes out in the middle of a chilly night, you wake up freezing. Then you must fan the flame and rekindle the fire. When your motivation runs low, rekindle your passion. Ask God to give you fresh fire. John the Baptist talked about being "baptize[d] with the Holy Spirit and with fire" (Matthew 3:11). Read the Word of God daily and spend time in prayer to fan into flame the fire of God in your soul. Get around leaders who will stir up your creativity and passion. Go to church on Sundays and worship with others to rekindle the fire.

Choose to succeed with or without anyone's assistance. Your success isn't dependent on anything but God. You and God are a winning majority! Leadership is lonely at times, but that's what makes true leaders—they are self-starters. Joshua told the people of Israel, "Choose for yourselves this day whom you will serve. . . . But as for me and my household, we will serve the Lord" (Joshua 24:15). Regardless of what others decide, you need to say, "But as for me. . . ." When you are decisive in your goals, you will inspire others just as Joshua did. The Israelites said, "Far be it from us to forsake the Lord to serve other gods!" (v. 16).

God has given you everything you need to succeed. Set your sights high, dream big dreams, write them down, and go forward with passion and perseverance. When the way gets difficult, get yourself fired up again to pressing on toward the goal, and don't stop until you reach the end. When you feel tired, get distracted, or question yourself, ignore those inner feelings and fan into flame the gift of God within you. Press forward with God's help and for His glory.

Life goals come from within your heart. People can't set your goals for you. Parents, pastors, and counselors can help you match your talents with your calling and give you guidance, but you need to decide what you are going to do with your life. No one can live your life for you.

Wise counselors will help us pursue the dreams that are already in our heart. They will empower us to live independently, not make us codependent on them. Codependency is an unhealthy relationship between someone who is needy and someone who wants to feel important. It takes a controlling person and somebody who likes the comfort of being controlled. If you think that sounds dysfunctional, you're right! Codependency is dysfunctional, so avoid such relationships and stand on your own two feet. Remember, you and God are a majority!

Progress Reports

Progress reports are important to see how far we've come and how much further we need to go. Progress reports evaluate our effectiveness and reward us for our accomplishments. When we fall behind in our progress, we must readjust our time frame and get back on track. Life is fluid. Things change, so we need to readjust our goals. Life consists of what we plan and what actually happens. Adjustments are normal and should not be seen as setbacks.

If you're getting in shape, write down your calories every day. Stay within the numbers allowed on your plan. Monitor your weight every day. Remember, the numbers don't lie (and neither does the mirror!). Measure the calories burned with every aerobics and strength-training workout. Weight loss and physical conditioning can be discouraging at times. Stay the course to reach your goal.

If you're working on financial goals, review your financial statements and monitor your progress. If you're working on a relationship, whether it be marriage or with parenting, write down the goals and track your progress. Celebrate your successes every step of the way. Success is the greatest motivator! When you succeed, you'll develop a winner's attitude in every area of life.

Willpower

Desire plus discipline equals success—"want power" plus willpower! *Willpower* is the ability to control or discipline yourself to do something positive or to avoid something negative. *Want power* is the all-consuming desire to succeed. So, want power plus willpower equals success.

We can have willpower in one area of our lives but lack it in another. We can be disciplined in some things but undisciplined in other things. Willpower means exercising discipline over desire. Our decisions must override our desires if we want to succeed. Our mind must rule over our emotions. *Willpower*, in Jesus' words, means "self-denial": "If anyone would come after me, he must deny himself and take up his cross daily and follow me" (Luke 9:23). So, we function whether we feel like it or not.

After Paul listed the fruit of the Spirit, he added, "Those who belong to Christ Jesus have crucified the sinful nature with its passions and desires" (Galatians 5:24). When something dies, it has no power over us. Crucifying the flesh means to rule over our basic impulses. When we show self-control, we cease being victims of desires, temptations, or peer pressure. When we govern our desires, we guarantee our destiny. Willpower gives us control of our own life.

Compare your life to a car. When you drive your car, other people are passengers going along for the ride. You are in the driver's seat. The passengers may be "backseat drivers," but you are the only one driving. You are in control. So it is with your life. Self-control puts you in the driver's seat. The driver decides the destination of the car, not the passengers. Who's driving your car? It's time for you to get in the driver's seat and decide where you want to go!

Excuses weaken our character and diminish our potential. One very common excuse is blaming our biology. Psychologists call it *biological determinism*. People justify and rationalize their weaknesses and sins, believing they were "born that way." Well, everybody is born the way they are, but that's not a legitimate excuse for irresponsibility. Biology isn't the root cause of everything in our life. We are spirit, mind, and body. We are all born with a sinful nature, but Jesus redeems us from sin so we can live a righteous life—living in right standing with God and others. The good news of Jesus is the promise that we can change! Grace means we don't have to stay the same. "If anyone is in Christ, [they are] a new creation" (2 Corinthians 5:17).

The greatest form of government is self-government, whereby we exercise the power of self-control. The opposite of self-control is living out of control. When Jesus rules in our hearts as Lord, we are no longer controlled by sinful desires or selfish impulses, so "in your hearts [always] set apart Christ as Lord" (1 Peter 3:15). Self-control is the power to exert your will over your emotions, desires, and impulses. Christ in us gives us the power to govern ourselves so we glorify God in all we do and say.

Jesus said, "If anyone chooses to do God's will, he will find out whether my teaching comes from God or whether I speak on my own" (John 7:17). The *New King James Version* reads, "If anyone wills to do His will. . . ." We *will* to do God's *will*. We purpose to do God's purpose. We plan to do God's plan. What we will to do is more important than what we feel. The fruit of self-control is produced in our lives when we submit to Christ's lordship and choose obedience to His will.

Marshmallow Test

A study done by the American Psychological Association provides insights about people's ability to reach their goals. A lack of discipline was cited by 70 percent of the people as the reason for not reaching their goals. While other factors can keep us from reaching our goals, the most common reason is the lack of self-discipline.

Various psychological studies show self-discipline results in better academic performance. The studies show a self-discipline in youth is a better indicator of later academic success than their IQ score. When a person possesses self-discipline, they will succeed. Parents, then, need to focus on cultivating self-discipline in their children by setting boundaries, giving them rules, and teaching them healthy study and life habits with household chores, time schedules, and consistent church attendance. Parents need to require good study habits at school, assist kids with their homework, and push them toward academic achievement while respecting each child's unique ability, interests, and aptitude.

A famous psychological test was conducted in the 1970s by Dr. Walter Mischel. *The marshmallow test* evaluated kids in school on their academic performance. The kids, in a test setting in a classroom, were given a plate of marshmallows and told, "Now you have two choices. You can eat the treat now and enjoy it. Or, if you wait until later today, you will get two treats." Then the researchers left the room.

They found mixed results. A lot of the kids went ahead and ate the marshmallow treat—they couldn't resist the urge. The kids who resisted the urge got two treats later in the day. After the series of tests were done, they started tracking the students' academic performance. They found the kids who delayed gratification, who waited for the two treats, always had better grades. They did better in school because they had self-control.

Self-discipline today will enrich your future. When you master your urges, you climb higher and go further in life than the undisciplined who spend their days floundering instead of focusing. Get your mind off the thing that tempts you and focus on the things that transform you into the best version of you.

Joseph was one of the most remarkable persons in the Old Testament. He ended up in Egypt because his brothers rejected him and sold him as a slave. He worked as a servant in the house of a man named Potiphar, who was a military leader and a political adviser in Egypt. Joseph distinguished himself as an honorable young man, so he earned Potiphar's respect and favor. (By the way, favor isn't something people give us but a reward we earn by hard work and integrity.)

Potiphar's wife was attracted to Joseph. She pursued an affair with him. She dressed seductively around the house to get Joseph's attention. She went so far to ask him directly to have an affair with her, but he refused her advances. One day when they were in the house alone, she caught him by his coat and said, "Come to bed with me!" At that moment, Joseph stood at a crossroad of desire and discipline. What would he do? "He left his cloak in her hand and ran out of the house" (Genesis 39:12).

When Joseph ran away from her demand, he ran toward his destiny! He was tempted to stay, but he ran. Joseph chose victory over vice, spirituality over sensuality, and the eternal over the immediate. That's the meaning and power of self-control the Holy Spirit will give us when we face temptations and trials. We only need to pray and depend on the Spirit's power when we stand at the crossroad of desire and discipline.

Self-control requires us to consider the results of our actions. Consider the good and the bad consequences. Decisions made in haste or in the heat of the moment can generate long-range results. So, before making a big decision, ask yourself about the upside and downside of your decision. What is the best-case scenario, and what is the worst-case scenario? Good decisions are godly decisions guided by eternal principles, not emotional passions.

Self-control brings great blessings. Joseph was blessed greatly by God because he ran when he was tempted to stay. The right choice results in happiness and health, prosperity and peace, promotion and success. Research shows people who practice self-discipline enjoy better mental health and physical health. They experience better relationships because they keep emotions and words under control and don't overreact at critical moments.

Keep Growing

Self-control comes from spiritual growth. The fruit of the Spirit is like growing natural fruit. It takes time to plant, nurture, and harvest fruit. Spiritual growth in the image of Jesus is an ongoing process. "For those God foreknew he also predestined to be conformed to the likeness of his Son" (Romans 8:29). God's will for us is to be conformed—shaped and molded—in the likeness of Jesus.

When you practice self-control, you will be victorious in life and never the victim of life's pressures, people's manipulation, or your own desires. The power of the Holy Spirit will enable you to run away from the things that are an obstacle to God's purpose in your life and run toward your divine destiny.

Someone once asked the master painter Rembrandt at what point a painting is complete. He responded, "A painting is finished when it expresses the intent of the artist."

God isn't finished with you yet, so keep growing fruit! The Christian life is not about perfection but progress. Keep learning, growing, and bearing fruit that will last so others may see "Christ in you, the hope of glory" (Colossians 1:27).